WALKING

PENDLE
and the
RIBBLE

Paul Hannon

HILLSIDE

HILLSIDE GUIDES - ACROSS THE NORTH

• •

WALKING COUNTRY

PENDLE
and the
RIBBLE

Paul Hannon

HILLSIDE

HILLSIDE
PUBLICATIONS
11 Nessfield Grove
Keighley
West Yorkshire
BD22 6NU

First published 1995

© Paul Hannon 1995

ISBN 1 870141 32 6

Cover illustration: Downham
Back cover: Pendle Hill; Newchurch;
Across the Ribble Valley from Pendle;
River Hodder at Cromwell's Bridge
(Paul Hannon/Big Country Picture Library)

Page One: Barrowford Toll House
Page Three: Witches Galore, Newchurch

Printed in Great Britain by
Joseph Ward Colourprint Ltd
Wesley Place
Dewsbury
West Yorkshire
WF13 1HR

CONTENTS

INTRODUCTION

At the heart of Lancashire its most famous hill and major river form an inseparable pairing, as the Ribble flows for many a lovely mile with mighty Pendle watching over. To folk east of the hill it is theirs, particularly as it overlooks the 'witch country' villages, but it is held in equally high regard by the townsfolk of Clitheroe, as a constant backdrop to their daily lives. While government boundaries may split them, no-one else would possibly see fit to do so.

The Ribble extends from wild heights in the Yorkshire Dales down to the sea beyond Preston, but the term Ribble Valley is commonly appended to the section both up- and down-stream of Clitheroe. The extent of Pendle Hill is even clearer, for this great mass is defined by a necklace of lovely villages around its base. Barley and Newchurch repose in the undulating folds at the foot of its very lap; while delectable Downham looks directly up to the Big End. Villages of the Ribble Valley, including Waddington, West Bradford, Grindleton and Sawley, all pay homage from a little further afield.

A rich contrast in walking alternates lush riverbanks with high windswept moorlands. Aside from Pendle, open country is found on both Waddington and Longridge Fells, while the Ribble is ably supported by the lower reaches of the Hodder and the Calder. Our walks touch very much on the fringes of adjacent Bowland, for the two merge happily in this corner of rural Lancashire. The Forest of Bowland Area of Outstanding Natural Beauty may be based on that great upland mass to the west, but its boundaries absorb many surrounding villages. Indeed, an entirely detached section takes in the environs of Pendle Hill. As a result, three-quarters of the walks in this book step through the AONB, many from start to finish.

Sawley Abbey

WALKING COUNTRY - PENDLE & THE RIBBLE

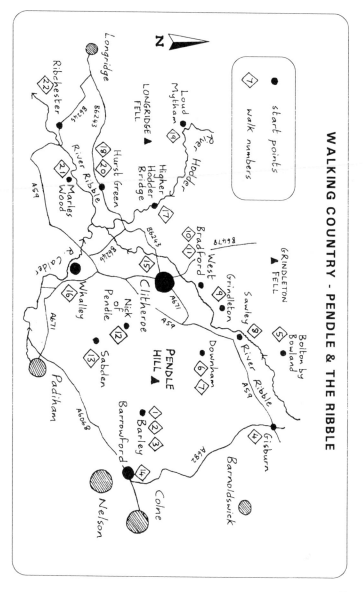

An attractive sign on the edge of Longridge Fell (WALK 20)

History abounds, most famously at the monastic sites of Whalley and Sawley, and also at Clitheroe Castle. Many fine old houses, with dark mullioned windows and weathered datestones reaching back through the centuries are encountered, as are more modest weavers' cottages and remains of industrial activity that reached these hitherto quiet villages. Today they are on the visitor's trail, and the likes of Downham, Waddington and Bolton by Bowland are as fair as any in the land.

While Pendle may indeed be indelibly linked with the Ribble, it claims a far more sinister connection. It all happened in a small area in the eastern shadow of the hill. The events of 1612 have been glamorised into the classic witch story of the north, and the subject of several novels. It began with a young girl suspected of foul play, quickly spread to her family, involved the local magistrate Squire Nowell of Read Hall, and resulted in an extended group being taken to Lancaster for trial and subsequent hanging. The very names of the supposed ringleaders strike a chill on a mist-wreathed day on Pendle. The surprise catch among the likes of Old Demdike and Old Chattox was Alice Nutter, a 'respectable' lady from Roughlee Hall.

Pendle Forest was established as an 11th century hunting forest covering the country south from the hill towards Colne. The hill has for centuries also been a beacon site, when a chain of fires would warn of approaching danger. Its busiest day might well be Good Friday, when it seems the whole of East Lancashire pulls on its boots to take Bank Holiday exercise. Needless to say, Hallowe'en is also a busy time for revellers. The hill is parcelled into numerous moors, though anyone up there is quite simply 'on Pendle'. Pendle's influence is such that even when seemingly far from it, every walk in the book reveals the hill at some stage.

Since 1974 the whole of this area has been administered by Lancashire County Council, but there are many who still regard themselves as Yorkshire folk. Centuries of history can't be dismissed at the stroke of a pen, and it is worth being aware that the whole of the west bank of the Ribble, as far south as its confluence with the Hodder, is true Yorkshire.

8

Clitheroe

This bustling market town is at the heart of a vast rural area. Focal point is the castle remains. The Norman keep watches over both town and valley from the natural motte of its limestone knoll. Open to visitors, the climb to the top is rewarded with a superb Ribble Valley prospect featuring the brooding mass of Pendle. This one situation perfectly encapsulates Clitheroe's setting at the heart of our area. Within the castle grounds a museum exhibits much of local interest, while Clitheroe Castle Fayre takes place annually, with mock battles amongst its attractions. The church of St. Mary Magdalene boasts a 15th century tower, while on the edge of town is the acclaimed geological trail at Salthill Quarry.

Getting around

The area is ideally placed for the Lancashire, and indeed many West Yorkshire, conurbations. It is also largely well served by public transport, and a brief comment on availability is given at the start of each walk. In 1994 the Ribble Valley line re-opened on a five year experiment, running between Blackburn and Clitheroe. Three new stations have been opened, including Whalley and Clitheroe itself.

Using the guide

Each walk is self-contained, essential information being followed by a simple map and concise description of the route. Dovetailed between are useful notes of features along the way, and interspersed are illustrations which capture the flavour of the walks and document many of the items of interest. The sketch maps identify the location of the routes rather than the fine detail, and whilst the description should be sufficient to guide one around, an Ordnance Survey map is recommended. The route as depicted can easily be plotted on the relevant OS map: all the walks are conveniently found on Landranger sheet 103, Blackburn & Burnley. To gain the most from a walk, however, the remarkable detail of the Pathfinder maps cannot be matched. They also serve to vary walks as desired, giving an improved picture of one's surroundings and the availability of linking paths. The following sheets serve the walks:

660 Slaidburn & Forest of Bowland: 5
661 Skipton & Hellifield: 4;5   **681** Burnley: 1;3;13;14
669 Clitheroe & Chipping: 1;5;6;7;8;9;10;11;12;15;17;19;20
670 Barnoldswick & Earby: 1;2;3;4;5;6;7;8;12;14
680 Longridge & Great Harwood: 1;12;13;15;16;17;18;20;21;22
Outdoor Leisure Map 21 - South Pennines: The extended 1995 edition entirely replaces sheets 670 and 681, and serves 1;2;3;4;5;6;7;13
Another useful map is *Paths around Pendle*, available locally. The following walks are entirely covered by it - 1;2;3;6;7;12;13

PENDLE HILL
from Barley

START Barley   Grid ref. SD 822403

DISTANCE 4½ miles

ORDNANCE SURVEY MAPS
1:50,000
Landranger 103 - Blackburn & Burnley
1:25,000
Outdoor Leisure 21 - South Pennines (1995 edition replaces
four individual Pathfinder sheets - 669,670,680,681)
or
Paths around Pendle footpath map also covers the whole
route

ACCESS Start from the village centre: large car park. Served
by infrequent buses from Nelson, Burnley and Clitheroe.

*Barley is an unassuming village that bears the brunt of Pendle-
seekers, though with a stream for kids to dabble in, and ice creams
on offer, there is every chance old Pendle will be forgotten. There
is a pub, the* Pendle Inn, *and a restaurant, as well as a Post office/
store. An information centre at the car park is open in season and
at winter weekends, also serving refreshments. There are public
toilets alongside. The car park occupies the site of an old mill dam,
for being near the larger settlements the village was caught up in
the Industrial Revolution: cotton factories and earlier small scale
handloom weaving mean't this was a busy little spot.*

☐ ***Cross the road from the picnic site and head along the lane past
the village hall at Barley Green.*** *A cotton mill that stood here was
destroyed by floods in 1880, and replaced with great irony by
Nelson's waterworks: our road passes their 1912 filter house.* ***The
road runs on to rise to the dam of Lower Ogden Reservoir. Here the***

road loses its surface, and continues the full length of the reservoir. Ahead, Spence Moor rises high above the upper dam, while Pendle's immediate moorland slopes look suitably impressive.

The lower reservoir was completed in 1914, its surface area takes in 21 acres and it is 59ft deep. **At the end the track rises beneath a plantation, then forks. Keep straight on for the upper dale, again rising up its right side to the foot of Upper Ogden Reservoir.** *This was opened eight years before its lower neighbour: though embracing only 7 acres it is of similar depth, such is its location in the deep-cut upper reaches of the valley.* **Now a footpath takes over along this northern shore, soon crossing the reservoir boundary wall and resuming outside.** *Here begins a super walk along the clough, immediately beyond the reservoir head giving a feeling of being really away from it all. From Upper Ogden Reservoir to the summit, the walk follows a concessionary route negotiated by North West Water.*

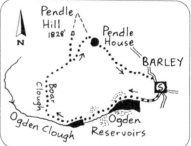

Beyond a ladder-stile in a descending wall the moor proper is reached, with much bracken on these lower slopes. Here the path climbs right a little before contouring on to approach Boar Clough. *This has long been known locally as the more appealing Whinberry Clough.* **Ford it and ignore a short-cut up to the right. Just a little further, Pendle Way signs point us up to the right, a short steeper pull above the clough - now on a thinner path - leading quickly to easier ground.** *We are now amid wilder, open moorland that could be almost anywhere: certainly the Pendle Way signs appear rather obtrusive up here.* **This super path rises ever gradually, leaving the bracken behind and approaching the now insignificant clough. The tinkling stream is soon forded, and the path bears away with a feeder on the right.**

Regular cairns confirm the clear route, whose gradients remain gentle throughout. *Views open out to the left to bring in Longridge Fell, Beacon Fell and the Bowland hills of Parlick and Fair Snape Fell.* **The path runs on towards a guidepost just short of the eastern scarp. This sends us up to the left, the path rising to a big pile of stones. By now the edge is only yards away, and the final, short**

pull can be savoured in the joy of the dramatic eastern view over this steep plunge. The trig. point (S2161) quickly appears ahead, and the climb is over. The likelihood is that there will be many folk up here, for almost everyone uses the 'tourist' path (see below), usually both up and down. First reward is a perch on the rim of the mighty drop, enjoying a bird's-eye view over Barley as it nestles in its fold of the hills. Pendle's isolation ensures extensive views in all directions, with the South and West Pennine moors beyond the East Lancashire conurbations, and a long Dales line-up to the north. Bowland, to the west, is merely a skyline, but is revealed in far greater fashion in both other featured ascents of the hill.

In poor conditions the 'tourist' route is the easiest descent: head north towards the prominent wall. Here the main highway, strengthened to counter the thousands of feet, reveals itself and slants down to the foot of the fell. **The suggested route leave by heading south along the edge - the path being just in from the edge. Beyond a big pile of stones it descends towards a guidepost. Just before, bear left along a green trackway that curves around to the top of the edge. Here the track becomes immediately stony and worn, slanting back down the fellside in good shape to meet the steep tourist path at the fell-gate.**

At a gate, slant across behind Pendle House to a stile from where the thin path descends the field to a gate. Bear right down the next field to a stile part-way down, and a little path runs down to the white-fronted Brown House. Go straight ahead to an old iron

kissing-gate, and resume down the field-side on a lovely path by a tiny stream. This becomes enclosed at the bottom. A nice pond on the right is a trout fishery. Emerging onto a lane go left a short way, then at a bend take a wooden footbridge on the right. Turn down the field, which proves to be the final one as the rooftops of Barley appear just ahead. At the far corner is a footbridge before the path becomes enclosed for the final yards back onto the main street.

*Cairn overlooking
Boar Clough*

2

TWISTON MOOR

START Barley   Grid ref. SD 822403

DISTANCE 7 miles

ORDNANCE SURVEY MAPS
1:50,000
Landranger 103 - Blackburn & Burnley
1:25,000
Pathfinder 670 - Barnoldswick & Earby *or*
Outdoor Leisure 21 - South Pennines (1995 edition) *or*
Paths around Pendle footpath map

ACCESS Start from the village centre. There is a large car park. Served by buses from Nelson, Burnley and Clitheroe.

For a note on Barley, please refer to page 10.

☐ *Head up the main street towards the Post office, and when the road swings sharp left out of the village, go straight ahead along a rough lane. This rises to the dam of Lower Black Moss Reservoir, then runs along the shore.* This sheet of water, constructed in 1903, makes a good foreground to the classic profile of Pendle's Big End. *At a fork beyond the reservoir, go right to climb to the dam of Upper Black Moss Reservoir (1894), and resume outside its bank. At the end the track crosses the inflow and runs out onto a road. Cross over and up the Mountain farm drive. When it swings away to a cattle-grid, keep straight on up the tiny beck-side to a stile at the end. Bear left in this big field, crossing the tiny beck and continuing to a row of trees. From a stile by a short length of wall, slant up the field to the far corner. Here are two stiles, yards short of the corner in each wall. Take that on the right, and head off on a very gradual wall-side pull over reedy Twiston Moor.*

Across to the left Pendle is magnificent now, while as the brow is gained, the Bowland moors are revealed beyond the Ribble Valley. Descending, when a wall appears ahead bear left to a gate in it.

Descend the field a little to a prominent bank, and here take a sojourn. This is a super moment, England's green and pleasant land as richly outspread as anywhere. The patchwork fields of the Ribble Valley lead to Longridge Fell, Bowland, and the peaks of the Yorkshire Dales, with the Craven area merging over to the right.

Turn right along this bank, to a wall-stile onto the bend of a green lane. Turn down it, at another bend running down above a wooded gill. At the bottom a surfaced drive is joined. Turn right, crossing the beck and leaving at once by a stile on the right. Just ahead is the fine old house of Clough Head (1702), and on the grass before it is the conspicuous Bulcock monument, with many inscriptions set into it.

From the stile slant gently up the bank and cross to a stile in a wall corner. Over it, turn straight up the wall-side for a reedy pull (regaining our lost height) that leads to a stile at the top onto the rough grass of Rimington Moor. Now go left, keeping near the wall and still enjoying those lovely views. Reaching sheep pens at the far end, take a big slab wall-stile on the left, advance a few yards, then use another to re-enter reedy pasture beyond the pens. Head up to the right and curve left to a wall corner, then follow the wall away. Ahead, a sunken way rising by a wall to the moortop will be our way. At the end take a stile in a facing wall, then cross to the foot of the sunken way and shadow it up to the very top corner.

Through a stile by the gate, advance a little further to the highest point of the walk, only marginally beneath the summit of the great horseshoe of Burn Moor. As the wall turns away to the left, go straight ahead on an old trackway that once served the former farm of Firber House down to the right. This grassy way runs on through the pasture, curving through a shallow saddle to meet a wall opposite. Ignore a stile midway, and keep on to a gate in a kink. Through it the clear track descends. Ahead are sweeping views

14

south over easternmost Lancashire, over Colne and Blacko Tower to the South Pennines dominated by Boulsworth Hill. *This track winds down to meet a farm track, which is followed right to slant down through the fields onto a quiet road.*

Here the walk's only farm can be omitted by turning up the road for ten minutes, regaining the route by the house at Stang Top. Otherwise, cross straight over and along the drive to Briercliffe. Head straight along the yard, and take a clever stile immediately after the last building on the right. Continue to the end, where there is a gap-stile by a gate. Turn down a few yards then cross straight over the field to a house. Just to its left is a stile by a gate, and a short enclosed way leading directly onto the front lawn. Pass the front of the house (the footpath pre-dates the house) and onto the drive. Instead of heading up it, however, take a hand-gate on the left and slant down to a wall-stile. From there rise to a wall corner, and follow the wall up to a crumbled ruin. Here turn sharp right to cross towards the house of Stang Top, joining the lane in front of it at a gate.

Turn left over the brow of the narrow lane, then take a gate on the right. This admits to the tame Stang Top Moor. Follow the trackway to the left, passing beneath the OS column (S4705) sat above an old quarry. Keep left on the main track at a fork and slant down the field, becoming ever fainter to approach the bottom corner. A little beyond an optional stile is a bridle-gate, from where a thin path descends through new plantings to the bottom corner. Here it runs, enclosed by greenery, down to an outdoor centre. This is White Hough Camp School, run for several decades now by Lancashire Education Authority: its cabins have been visible for some while.

Continue down the drive to the hamlet of White Hough. As the road swings sharp left in front of the beck, turn right along a broad track. This is the old road to Barley, and runs upstream in grand surrounds. En route at Narrowgates, two attractive rows of former weavers' cottages, restored in the 1970's, precede what remains of the cotton mill, closed in the 1960's. Note the preserved stone square chimney. *Just beyond the old mill, a path goes straight forward to re-enter the car park.*

Bulcock Monument, Clough Head

3

WITCH COUNTRY

START   Barley   Grid ref. SD 822403

DISTANCE   5 miles

ORDNANCE SURVEY MAPS
1:50,000
Landranger 103 - Blackburn & Burnley
1:25,000
Outdoor Leisure 21 - South Pennines (1995 edition) replaces
Pathfinders 670, 681 *or*
Paths around Pendle map also covers the whole route

ACCESS Start from the village centre: large car park. Served
by infrequent buses from Nelson, Burnley and Clitheroe.

For a note on Barley please refer to page 10.

❏ *Cross the road from the picnic site and head along the lane past
the village hall at Barley Green. A cotton mill that stood here was
destroyed by floods in 1880, and replaced with great irony by
Nelson's waterworks: our road passes their 1912 filter house. The
road runs on to rise to the dam of Lower Ogden Reservoir. Here the
road loses its surface, and continues the full length of the reservoir.*
Ahead, Spence Moor rises high above the upper dam, while
Pendle's immediate moorland slopes look suitably impressive.

The lower reservoir was completed in 1914, its surface area takes
in 21 acres and it is 59ft deep. *At the end the track rises beneath
a plantation then forks. Keep straight on for the upper dale, again
rising up the right side of the dam to the foot of Upper Ogden
Reservoir.* This was opened eight years before its lower neighbour:
though embracing only 7 acres it is of similar depth, such is its
location in the deep-cut upper reaches of the valley.

Turn along the dam top. From the stile at the end, rough moorland is entered. A clear path slants up the reedy terrain to join a crumbling wall. Retrospective views rapidly unfold to reveal a superb profile of Pendle's eastern scarp rising beyond the reservoir, and also up into the recesses of Ogden Clough beneath Spence Moor. Four sheets of water are now in view as the Black Moss twosome beyond Barley appear. *The wall is traced up to the brow on Driver Height.* Five minutes reposing on a grassy patch here is time well spent. Ahead, the next stages of our route through the 'hidden valley' are revealed, but of greater merit is the last, lingering look back at the Pendle scene.

Continue down with the wall, soon emerging into a field to drop down to a narrow, winding road. For a short-cut, turn right for Lower Sabden Fold. Alternatively, on approaching the gate, turn right across the field, contouring along to follow a wall-top to a crumbling corner. Keep straight on, descending to a corner stile

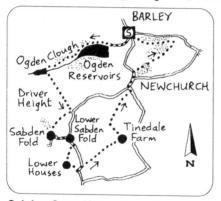

with Sabden Fold Farm ahead. Advance again towards the foot of wooded Cock Clough, turn down a green way before it. Down through several gates the way emerges alongside the buildings and out onto a lane. Narrow and winding, it runs along to the left to the hamlet of Lower Sabden Fold.

Turn down to the right here, passing sombre Sabden Great Hall, with mullioned and transomed windows and twin bays. *Just over the beck, take a stile on the right and cross three fields bound for Lower Houses Farm, ahead. A gap-stile in the corner admits to the yard between the buildings. Turn left along the front of the house and up the drive.* The attractive house front is inscribed 'MS HS 1592'. Back over to the right is a southern aspect of Spence Moor.

At the road turn left for 100 yards and then keep straight on the rough track alongside the buildings at Higher Town. A short-lived walled way at the end culminates in a potential quagmire before a pleasant wall-side stroll heads away. There are good views over the

Witches Galore, Newchurch

hidden valley now, with the ridge above and the cluster of Newchurch ahead. **From a good corner stile at the end, advance with a fence towards the next corner: here there is a short choice. A pathless short-cut slants across the large pasture below, keeping well to the right of a dangerously marshy tract in the reeds to join the track coming down from the right. The safer option is to keep straight on for Tinedale Farm, ahead. Past the main buildings, take the track down to the left.**

Picking up the short-cut, it runs on to approach the house at Bull Hole. Just before, at a gate, Pendle Way signs send us through a step-stile on the right, and follow the wall along the field-sides to Moss End. Passing left of the house, leave its drive after just a few yards and resume our direct line, slanting clearly up a field and on through a couple more to emerge onto the road opposite Newchurch school.

Turn up to the left, past mounting steps and the church to the junction in the centre. Whilst compiling this walk St. Mary's church was enjoying 450th anniversary celebrations, as its tower dates from 1544 (the rest is two centuries younger). Near the porch is the 'witch's grave', reputedly that of Alice Nutter. A rushbearing procession is held here in August. Also in this tiny hillside village is a seasonal tearoom, toilets, and 'Witches Galore', a unique shop. What is missing, however, is the Lamb Inn, which recently called

18

a final last orders: already this private house in the centre is unrecognisable as an inn. **Head up the main street, past the houses to a bend at the top.** *Mighty Pendle is revealed in all its glory, with Barley nestling below. Going straight down the road will see the walk finished in ten minutes.*

Otherwise, turn right along a drive, but leave almost at once by a stile in front, following the wall along the broad ridge-top outside the wood. Part-way along a stile admits into it, and a slanting path cuts a corner of the wood to pick up the Pendle Way again at a stile at the end. *The Pendle Way, incidentally, leaves the village down Jinny Lane, quickly taking a stile on the left to cross the field into the wood, there rising gradually to meet us here.*

Now cross to the wall on the left, and follow this down outside another small plantation. On reaching a clever corner-stile past an intervening one, the other side of the wall leads down the broad ridge-end to emerge onto a green track. *If things are muddy, you might cross straight over and down the last field onto the road: the track opposite leads past new houses at White Hough and follows the beck upstream into Barley (see WALK 2).* **Otherwise, turn left along this walled trackway, which runs on above Boothman Wood to eventually drop down into the village by way of the cottages at Bridge End.** *Pendle provides a final, memorable flourish.*

At Barley, looking to Pendle Hill

The Barley Mow RESTAURANT

4

BRACEWELL

START Gisburn   Grid ref. SD 830488

DISTANCE 6¼ miles

ORDNANCE SURVEY MAPS
1:50,000
Landranger 103 - Blackburn & Burnley
1:25,000
Outdoor Leisure 21 - South Pennines (1995 edition) replaces
Pathfinders 661 and 670

ACCESS Start from the village centre. There is a large
parking area at the eastern end, outside the former *Travellers
Hotel*. Clitheroe-Skipton buses run through here.

*Merely a ramble through the fields, but with lovely views, and the
attractions of Gisburne Park, Horton and Bracewell. Gisburn is a
street village that quakes to the rumble of the A59. Centrepiece is
the venerable church of St. Mary the Virgin. It boasts a Norman
tower, while some stonework in the nave came from Sawley
Abbey. It contains memorials to the Listers of Gisburne Park (later
the Lords Ribblesdale).* The Ribblesdale Arms *dates from 1635 -
note the inscription on its three-storeyed porch. There is a further
pub, three eating places and a Post office/store.*

☐ **From the church, head west along the main street and turn
right down the road to Bolton by Bowland past the auction mart and
toilets. The road crosses the Blackburn-Hellifield railway by the old
station.** *Along to the right, Gisburn Tunnel's castellated entrances
are evidence of the involvement of Lord Ribblesdale in not having
his park spoiled by the railway. Leaving the village behind, the road
affords sweeping views over the Ribble Valley, to Grindleton Fell
to the left, and far north to the fells of the Yorkshire Dales.*

The road descends past Deerhouse Farm, *with home-made dairy
ice cream and a picnic area.* **Delving into deep woodland, the road
runs down to Gisburn Bridge.** *This is a grand spot: two main arches*

*span the broad Ribble flowing through deep wooded surrounds.
Alongside is an old house sporting mullioned windows - note the
tablet on the side wall. **Don't cross the bridge, but double back to
the left of the house, and up a drive climbing through the trees.
Head past the house above, but as a branch runs on to Gisburne
Park, swing right with the main drive. At a fork beyond a cattle-grid
bear left, still on the main drive.** Over to the left is the big house
of Gisburne Park.*

*The impressive nine bay front dates from around 1750, and was
the former residence of Lord Ribblesdale: the first Lord is remembered for planting a million oak trees by the Ribble. The house
currently operates as a private hospital. **On joining its drive, our
way crosses straight over and down through trees to an arched
bridge on Stock Beck. As it runs along to a house, keep left on the
track outside it grounds, doubling back up the wooded bank.
Emerging, it runs pleasantly along to meet the Hellifield road.***

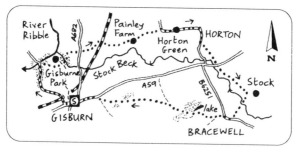

*Cross straight over, and from the gate (note the 1903 gatepost)
head across the pasture alongside a tiny stream. Where it runs
undergound, cross and aim for the far corner of the field. Here a
previously unseen underpass takes us beneath the railway. At the
other side, advance 50 yards with the fence then take a gate in it.
Follow it down a little, then bear left with another fence to a gate
in the far corner.** Over to the right is Weets Hill, with Pendle further
back. **Ahead is Painley Farm, and our way makes straight for it.***
*Depending upon the weather and the cows, entry into its yard may
be a sloppy affair. **Above the buildings its drive is joined, and leads
out through fields onto a narrow lane. Turn right, and follow its
meandering course to Horton in Craven.***

*En route to Horton the farm complex of Horton Green is passed, and
also the attractive mullioned facade and gable of Horton Hall up to
the left, the tiny stream making a nice foreground. **The lane climbs***

21

to reach the hamlet, and turns right through it. Note the Congregational chapel founded in 1670, with a dozen gravestones outside, slotted between two cottages. The last building on the right is a well presented farmstead.

Descending the lane, the mill chimneys and rooftops of Barnoldswick are prominent over to the left, while greater interest is provided by Weets Hill rising ahead. **The last buildings on the left are red brick barns: here take a stile and a few steps. Turn down the farmyard track, crossing to a gate into a small enclosure. Cross to the far side, where a stile in a fence sees us off alongside a line of trees on the right. Ahead now is the** Coronaton Hotel, **and beyond the fence corner keep straight on for it, going to the left to find a stile up onto the A59.**

The Coronation *is a long renowned watering hole on Blackpool coach trips. After a period in the doldrums it has re-opened with new enthusiasm. It is normally open for morning coffee, a useful halt to fortify for the road crossing.* **Directly opposite, a stile down the bank from a gate sees us into a lovely pasture alongside the meandering Stock Beck. This time it is followed upstream, though the path properly short-cuts the sweeping bend. At the end are a gate and stile in succession. Here, despite us later using a footbridge further upstream, we must desert the beck, for now.**

Aim away between fence and beck, slanting across the field to a solid stile part-way up the wall. Resume the slant up the field behind to reach the brow. *Over to the left are the scattered buildings of Stock, while to the right across the beck is Bracewell: this is a grand vantage point, with Weets Hill and Pendle Hill rising beyond.* **Turn down to the right outside the wooded area and descend towards the prominent footbridge.** *On the left is the site of an old quarry, while part of our descent is an old sunken trackway. The beck is in typically wispish mood.* **Beyond, advance to a stile, and climb the field-side outside a sunken old way.** *This original route has long been abandoned to undergrowth and waterlogging.* **At the top a gate admits onto the B6251 at Bracewell.**

Just to the left past the village hall is the old Post office. An inscription records the building and furnishing of rooms for the residence of a schoolmaster in the 19th century, with money arising from the sale of an organ: it is part-hidden by a newer porch. Centrepiece of the hamlet is the lovely old church of St. Michael. It has a leper's squint, and 'Mouseman' pews. Note the ridge-line of an earlier nave against the part-Norman tower. Outside the church is an arch that came from the old manor house.

Back on the road, turn right (west) for 200 yards, and at the sharp bend advance along a driveway. *Over to the left, Weets Hill towers as mightily as Pendle itself. As this swings left to Calf House Laithe, keep straight on the broad track. This runs past a large pond, profusely enjoyed by ducks and backed by woodland.*

Over a cattle-grid beyond it take a stile on the right, cross a footbridge and slant up the field. A novel wall-stile admits to the woodland enclosure behind. A slim path rises away to find a hurdle-stile at the top. Bear left over the top of this domed field, earning sweeping views. Cross to a fence corner, but instead of following the track away, trace the other side of the fence down towards the corner. Fifty yards along the wall to the left is a sturdy stile, from where head up the field to a wall-stile on the skyline. In the same direction, slant down towards the small beck across the field, where a stile indicates our route. Beyond, bear left to a stile in the fence descending from the modest Walter Hill Plantation, and continue to another. Slant up to the brow beyond the last trees.

Ahead, Gisburn returns to the scene, hidden beyond further trees. Bear left over the brow to the fence heading away, locating a stile a short way along it. Head away from it with a line of hawthorns, and at the end pass through two stiles in quick succession. A pronounced mound heads away with a sunken way. As it swings right to descend the field, maintain the slant down beneath a fence corner and continue down towards the A59. The road is joined at the start of a drive at the eastern end of the village.

St. Michael's,
Bracewell

5
BOLTON BY BOWLAND

START   Bolton by Bowland   Grid ref. SD 785494

DISTANCE   6 miles

ORDNANCE SURVEY MAPS
1:50,000
Landranger 103 - Blackburn & Burnley
1:25,000
Pathfinder 660 - Slaidburn & Forest of Bowland
        661 - Skipton & Hellifield (not important)
        669 - Clitheroe & Chipping
670 - Barnoldswick & Earby *or* Outdoor Leisure 21 (1995 edition)

ACCESS   Start from the village centre. There is a car park at
the western end, by Skirden Bridge. The village is served by
very occasional bus from Clitheroe via Gisburn.

*Bolton by Bowland is a hugely attractive village, off the beaten
track but popular with knowledgable visitors. It boasts two greens,
the smaller one with remains of a medieval cross and the old
stocks. Pride of place goes to the church of St Peter & St Paul, or
more correctly its tower. Dating from the 15th century, it is a
splendid edifice of a style not familiar to these parts. The church
itself was rebuilt in 1852, but contains much of older interest. In
particular seek out the remarkable 1460's memorial to Sir Ralph
Pudsay: 10ft long, it bears portraits of himself, 3 wives and 25
children, all carved in low relief. There is also a brass of Henry
Pudsay (1509) and wife, and a 16th century font bearing the arms
of numerous local landowning families, complete with a more
recent 'Mouseman' cover.*

*The Coach and Horses inn offers refreshment, while next to the
Post office is Primrose Cottage, with a 1716 datestone on its lintel.
There are toilets and a small information room at the car park: the
wall-mounted Pathfinder map centred on the village would solve
our edge of map problems if it would fit in a pocket!*

❑ *Cross the bridge by the car park and from a stile turn upstream to shadow Skirden Beck through pleasant surrounds. After a couple of stiles in quick succession a steep wooded bank materialises, and on the dangerously eroded brow a magnificent prospect of the winding beck is enjoyed. Here too we are deflected away from it by the bank, though soon the trees relent and further good views obtained as our natural line runs along to a stile between hollies. Cross the next large pasture towards a nursery, being deflected by a tiny stream to a stile, from where a small enclosure alongside the nursery sees us up to a stile onto a road.*

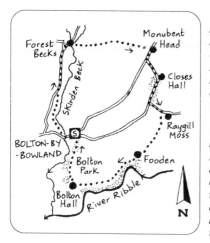

Turn right along this quiet road, passing the lone house of Stoop Lane. Its especially attractive porch bears a 1703 datestone. **Beyond, the road swings down to Forest Becks.** *This tiny hamlet is named where the two principal becks of the ancient Gisburn Forest meet. Here re-cross Skirden Beck, once again in pleasant surrounds.* **Immediately over the bridge, turn along the cart track past cottages on the right to a bridge over Monubent Beck, just above the confluence.**

Don't go striding off up the track, but at once take a gate into the trees. Here a seldom tramped green way slants up above the track, swinging left at the top to run on through the trees. This is the start of Monubent Lane. With the house at Hill Top visible over to the right, turn onto the hollowed way on the left and head on through a gate. Part-sunken and embowered in trees the way runs on through another gate and the quality improves. This idyllic section exemplifies the delights of an old lane surviving in such condition: hollies abound, and in late autumn, oakleafs carpet the floor. **The inevitable happens when a modern track takes over - though the way seems barred, a gate round to the left gives access. Resume along this track,** *pleasant enough but no longer 'special'. Passing the converted house at Little Monubent, the views open out: over to the right is the prow of Pendle Hill.*

At the end debouch onto a road opposite Monubent Head Farm, and turn right. The Grindleton Fell massif is prominent over to the right. A junction at Stump Cross is quickly reached. In the edge of the garden note the cross, a modern replacement in what seems to be an original base. Go left here along the narrow Stump Cross Lane, passing the extensive farm complex at Closes Hall. Note the interesting architecture of the farm itself (1895 date). Roman-like, our lane runs on past overgrown parkland woods to a junction with the Gisburn road at Closes Hall Lodge. Turn left a short way.

Just short of the farm buildings at Raygill Moss, ignore the stile and footpath sign and continue a little nearer the buildings. A path actually crosses the road here: turn through the gate on the right, and head away with a fence on the right. An intervening fence is stepped over, then all is plain sailing as the original fence remains a constant companion, swinging away to the right and taking in several small kinks to finally reach a corner. Take the gate in front, and continue away with a fence now on the left. Ahead, the farmstead at Fooden soon appears.

With a deep-cut stream coming in for company, a track forms to descend to the bottom of the yard. Turn up to the right on the main track between the buildings. One old house is passed left, before rising straight up the upper yard past Fooden Hall. This lovely 17th century building has a two-storey gabled porch and mullioned windows.

St. Peter & St. Paul,
Bolton by Bowland

26

At the top of the yard is a gate bearing waymarks. Emerging into a field, turn left outside the buildings, returning to the confines at a gate, then swinging right to head away to another gate, and total escape. Advance along the field bottom on a part-sunken green way, and in the field running atop a wooded bank falling steeply to the Ribble Gorge. The river is heard below, though only the bare trees of winter help see it. At the next stile we emerge into open pasture above the gorge, running on a most enjoyable enclosed way between fences. With luck, a herd of roe deer may be roaming in this neighbourhood. At the very end, well beneath the buildings of Scott Laithe, cross to the next prominent stile across the field, and likewise with the buildings that remain at Bolton Hall in view ahead. Keep straight on for them to reach a gateway in the enclosing wall. Turn right along the track, dropping down to the edge of the houses.

*Henry VI found refuge in the original Bolton Hall after the Battle of Hexham in 1464. For more than four centuries it was the home of the Pudsay family. Today even its replacement of 1806 has gone, having been demolished in the 1960's. **Turn right on the drive out: this returns directly to the village centre, opposite the church.** En route we pass a fallen stone commemorating the planting of a Coronation Oak for George V in 1911, while at a small cutting on the brow is a former cross. The base remains, upon a larger plinth. Over to the left is a sizeable crag. The final stage is as good as anything yet, with a lovely prospect of Skirden Beck winding down from the village. With the church tower beckoning, a stately avenue of oaks see us out onto the road.*

Village stocks and Cross, Bolton by Bowland

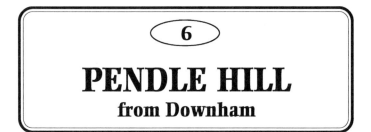

6

PENDLE HILL
from Downham

START Downham   Grid ref. SD 785442

DISTANCE 5½ miles

ORDNANCE SURVEY MAPS
1:50,000
Landranger 103 - Blackburn & Burnley
1:25,000
Pathfinder 669 - Clitheroe & Chipping
          670 - Barnoldswick & Earby
NB: Outdoor Leisure 21 - South Pennines (1995 edition)
replaces sheet 670 **or**
Paths around Pendle footpath map covers the whole route

ACCESS Start from the village centre. There is a car park at
the bottom of the village. Downham is served by bus from
Clitheroe.

*This is unquestionably the connoisseur's route over Pendle. Note
that both the ascent and descent routes are not public rights of
way, but concessionary paths negotiated with landowners. For
notes on Downham please refer to page 33.*

☐ **From the bridge at the bottom of the village, turn back along the
side road to the car park entrance. Between road and entrance, turn
up a short drive to a couple of houses. Take a stile by a gate
between them, and head off with a fence on the right.** *Over to the
right is a good prospect of the rather grand Downham Hall.* **From
a gate at the end continue on outside a wood.** *Now there is ample
time to appraise the great bulk that is our objective, with Pendle's
Big End rising majestically: note also the big shelter and Scout Cairn
on Pendle's whaleback skyline.*

Emerging into a field with the limestone knoll of Worsaw Hill to the right, cross straight over to a fence corner, and on a little further to a three-slab corner stile. Cross the field bottom to a like stile, then on to a wall-corner and alongside the wall. Worsaw Hill displays increasing evidence of its limestone origins. *Just before reaching Worsaw End House, take a gate in the wall and turn down to join its drive. This leads out onto a lane.* Worsaw End was the setting for the acclaimed 1960's film Whistle Down the Wind.

Turn right along the lane, and at the second corner, where the road goes right, remain on the 'no through road' rising away. When it turns sharp left towards a farm, keep straight on up an enclosed green way. This delectable section is an old sheep droving way off the hill. Already there are sweeping views over to the Bowland fells. Note also Clitheroe Castle very prominent on its knoll, backed by Longridge Fell. Looking further north, Ingleborough is already in view. When the Scout Cairn finally disappears from view, the next time we see it things will be very different.

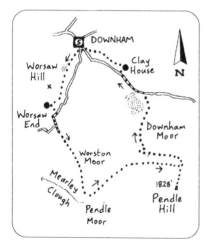

A stile at the top of the green way gives immediate access onto Pendle's slopes. Head directly up the right side of the deep-cut little ravine. As the going eases, the steep upper flank of the hill is revealed ahead, with our intended sunken way up to the right. Constantly increasing are the views out, though only in terms of greater distance rather than individual features, as most aspects of the Ribble Valley have long been visible.

Only a vague path crosses the gentler gradients of Worston Moor, but simply bear across to the right-hand wall: the reedy terrain is not the onerous prospect it first looks. At the wall corner advance along to the right a short way, then turn up the hugely prominent sunken way. This leads unfailingly up the steep flank, the upper section of which is superfluously marked by a string of cairns. The remnants of an old boundary wall are seen on

29

the stonier upper section. **Just before this point one can make a direct climb up the final slopes to arrive at the Scout Cairn.** *Those who missed the turning find the sunken way fades at the top, where cairns point the way back over easy ground to the Scout Cairn. Only on gaining the obelisk is its true size fully appreciated. It proves to be a well constructed 10ft pillar, a well known Ribble Valley landmark. The memorial tablets set into it explain its name.*

The ascent is virtually complete now: what remains is a splendid, high level moorland walk. **From the cairn advance north along an increasingly defined edge, passing a line of cairns to reach a massive stone shelter.** *Solidly built as recently as 1983, it is well furnished with seating. It is also well appreciated on the right day, and Pendle offers many such days.* **Just beyond is a ladder-stile in an equally sturdy wall.** *Down to the left is a boundary stone inscribed 'W', while fifty yards to the right another encased in the wall is inscribed 'D', with benchmark; and 'W' on the other side: these refer to Downham and Worston.*

More impressive is the view, the finest section of which is depicted below (fells beyond Bowland are in upper case). Our starting point is only one of numerous Ribble Valley villages now displayed as on a map. A clear day will bring in various sections of the skyline of Lakeland peaks. The southernmost, Black Combe, slots tidily in over the Trough of Bowland: its 1968ft summit is a neat 50 miles distant. The Scafell group reaches three or four miles further. Mention must also be made of the peaks of the Yorkshire Dales,

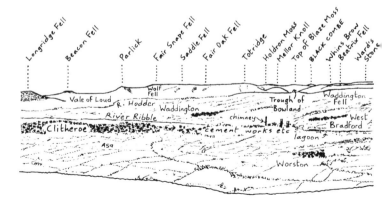

which further round from Ingleborough include parts of Wild Boar Fell, Widdale Fell, Great Shunner Fell, Penyghent, Plover Hill, Fountains Fell, Darnbrook Fell, Buckden Pike and Great Whernside. Back the other way, south of Bowland, a clear day also features the mountains of Snowdonia. Major omissions Helvellyn and Whernside are hidden by White Hill and Ingleborough respectively, though the Helvellyn group moves into place by the time the stile onto Downham Moor is gained beyond the shelter.

Here the main path bears right, now a superb green pathway across the lovely terrain of Downham Moor. An attractive little pool is quickly passed, and by now our summit also appears, the trig. point prominent atop peaty slopes. This delectable track offers a very easy final stage, still enjoying those outward views as we swing round to bring in the mountains and hills of the eastern Dales. **The track runs along to a ladder-stile, from where a broad yet faint way runs the final five minutes up to the waiting OS column (S2161).**

Arrival on a summit is always a good moment, and here we have the added bonus of the hitherto unseen view eastwards, over the great drop of the eastern scarp to the environs of Barley. There can be no day of the year when no-one ventures up here. For more on Pendle's summit, please refer to page 12.

Return to the wall, on a good day along the eastern scarp. The descent to Downham from the Big End has two beginnings. The unmarked one sets off from the ladder-stile, a few yards on our outward track before a thinner path keeps straight on across the

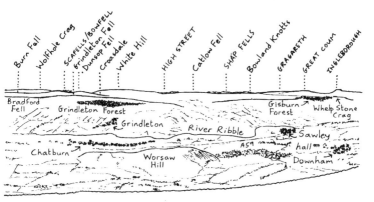

Bowland and beyond: across the Ribble Valley from the Scout Cairn

31

moor. This quickly broadens into an old grassy trackway, descending a little more and slanting down the great northern slopes. The acknowledged route turns down the wall-side a few yards to the top of the Barley path. The 'tourist' route up the hill gives the first-time visitor quite a shock to discover this man-made path starting from nothing! *Our way, however, takes the adjacent stile by a modern Pendle Way marker: this also confirms the route to Downham, and a grand path heads away.*

Within yards Downham appears directly ahead. **A steep descent leads to Fox's Well.** *This lively spring is named after Quaker founder George Fox, who climbed the hill in 1652 and here had his great vision that resulted in the founding of the Society of Friends, more commonly known as Quakers. Its older name is Robin Hood's Well. Fox recorded:* "As I went down I found a spring of water in the side of the hill, with which I refreshed myself...."

Beyond the spring the path narrows and very quickly turns to commence an extended contour around the northern slopes to join up with the broader descent path. Together they slant down, quickly reaching a great dog-leg which walkers are urged to make use of, thus preventing the obvious erosion of a direct short-cut. At the foot of the dog-leg the path turns directly down, a complete change of character now onto reedy moorland. The way remains clear all the way down. At an intervening fence-stile look back to see old quarries on the skyline, and their very pronounced service track raking up. *Eventually a stile leads off the moor. A faint path descends a rough pasture to a kissing-gate onto Pendle Road.*

Turn left down the lane, which leads within a mile or so back into Downham. An easy alternative forsakes the road at the first farm drive on the right (Look out for a new footpath diversion here). This doubles back a short way to enter the yard of Clay House. Go past the house, then left through a gateway into the field. Slant down to the bottom corner by the tree-lined beck. Only now does dogged Penyghent give up the ghost and disappear from view. *Just short of the corner a tight stile admits to the confines of the beck.*

Turn downstream, swapping banks at a small footbridge. After a couple of stiles an open pasture is entered. The chirpy stream meanders along to join Downham Beck. The houses are just ahead now, overtopped, even now, by Bowland's shapely Parlick Pike. *The beck leads pleasantly down past a bubbling spring to enter the village. A final stile leads into a lane, which leads out, with the intermittent beck, to the village centre.*

RIMINGTON

START Downham   Grid ref. SD 785442

DISTANCE 5¼ miles

ORDNANCE SURVEY MAPS
1:50,000
Landranger 103 - Blackburn & Burnley
1:25,000
Pathfinder 669 - Clitheroe & Chipping
670 - Barnoldswick & Earby *or* Outdoor Leisure 21 (1995 edition)
or Paths around Pendle footpath map covers the whole route

ACCESS Start from the village centre: car park at the bottom
of the village. Downham is served by bus from Clitheroe.

*Downham has few rivals in the 'prettiest village' stakes. Its street
climbs steeply from beck to church. St. Leonard's church was
restored in 1910, but the tower dates back much further. Inside are
monuments to the Assheton family who bought the manor in 1558.
The pub across the road bears their arms. Tucked round the corner
is Downham Hall: the Asshetons built the original in Elizabethan
times, though what is seen today largely dates from 1835. Also at
the top of the street is the Post office and cafe, while on the small
green out front are the remains of the village stocks.*

*At the bottom of the village ducks dabble in the stream: facing it
is 16th century Old Well Hall, a former manor house with a two-
storeyed gabled porch and mullioned windows. A third old hall is
found on the back lane from the car park to the main street.
Attractive cottages line the street, many once used by hand-loom
weavers. There are toilets and an information room at the car park.*

❑ *From the bridge climb the road towards the church. Take the
first right turn, and beyond the next junction advance only as far
as the last houses. On the left a pathway rises to a lone house. Go
up through the private looking gate and up the field-side. Through
a locally typical three-slab stile rise to the brow of the large pasture*

33

*known as **Downham Green**. A clear day reveals a super prospect up the Ribble Valley to the peaks of the Yorkshire Dales. As ever, the Ribblesdale pair of Ingleborough and Penyghent grab attention.*

Our way slants gently right now, dropping only gradually. A steeper drop is encountered and a way down through this is made, aiming for the prominent limestone knolls across to the right. Approaching them, the base of an old cross is encountered. *The socket is very distinct in what initially appears to be merely a rogue boulder.* **In front of the main, tree-topped outcrop, descend left past smaller ones to a stile in a hedge. On the other side is a driveway, and this leads along to the right to Downham Mill.** *Now a private dwelling, the arch of this former corn mill's undershot waterwheel hole is prominent.* **The path passes to the right of the house and out along a green trackway behind.** *An unofficial diversion may suggest using the field-bottoms on the near side of the house: it is bogus.*

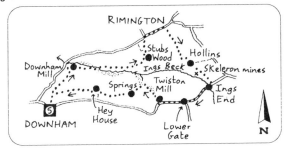

The track follows the old mill race up past its beginning at a small weir on the beck. In the corner just beyond is a stile, and the way continues upstream to a footbridge. Cross and resume upstream a short way before turning up to the left, passing beneath the scant remains of a limekiln. Climb the steep bank just past it to reach a fence at the top. Don't take the stile into the field, but turn right, outside the fence and along the top of the steep bank falling to the beck. High beyond it is the familiar outline of Pendle, a form that will become more familiar still during this walk. **On reaching the brow, cut a corner of the fence and slant down the bank to the far end, to find a side-stream and stile midway between the descending fence and the main beck. Scale the bank behind, climbing directly up the field on a thin trod to a fence corner at the top.**

There is a choice of ways here. The official path takes the right-hand stile towards the house above: midway, take a stile in the fence and cross to the far corner of the enclosure to a gate, then

follow the drive out from the house. *A courtesy path, avoiding the house, takes the left-hand stile and slants across the field to the bottom of a line of trees to find a step-stile in a fence corner. Cross this small enclosure to another by a gate opposite to join the drive, and the public footpath.* **Cross a stream by the drive, then leave by striking directly up the field. Bear well right of a lone house, through a gateway near the top and slant across to the far corner, where a stile gives access onto the road at Rimington.**

Turn right along the main street. *Passed are a local information board, an up-market womens' fashion store, and the* Black Bull *pub. Hymn-writer Francis Duckworth, best known for 'Rimington', lived here. Virtually all the houses - a very mixed hybrid - are spread along the north side of the road, facing Pendle's Big End.*

Keep on to the end, then opposite the last house take a rickety gate on the right. Climb directly up the field, bearing left towards the top to find a stile in the fence ahead, near the corner. Resume up past

a dewpond to a stile just right of a barn. *Look back now to appraise a Dales panorama, with Ingleborough and Penyghent joined by the very distinctive limestone hills above Settle.*

The stile admits to an old green way. From a redundant stile opposite advance 50 yards into the field, then go left to a stile back onto the green way. Follow this along to the right towards Hollins Farm. A field is crossed to gain it: a stile to the right of the house admits to the yard entrance.

Cross base and limestone knoll, above Downham Mill

Cross straight over to a stile ahead, from where a deep green track quickly rises to a stile. Alongside are the prominent remains of the Skeleron lead mines, featuring a series of grassed over spoil heaps and bell pits, with the main quarry colonised by trees just beyond. From this brow look back to survey a magnificent prospect. From west to east we have Longridge Fell, Beacon Fell, Parlick and the Bowland moors, Waddington and Grindleton Fells, northern Bowland, Whelp Stone Crag, Ingleborough, Penyghent, Rye Loaf Hill, Fountains Fell, Gordale Scar, Great Whernside, Meugher, and Cracoe Fell.

Beyond the stile the track runs on by a fence high above the deep cut side valley of Ings Beck. This marks the traditional Yorkshire-Lancashire boundary, with Pendle looming large across it. The flanks beneath us are seamed with old workings, almost entirely grassed over: this is a super section. A filled-in shaft is passed, just after which an old quarry sits by the track - note the tilted rock strata. **The track runs on to join a narrow lane. Turn down to the tiny hamlet of Ings End, and back up the other side. A junction is quickly reached.** Note another old quarry in the field in front. **Bear right, the lane soon descending.** High on the left are more substantial quarrying scars, while the massive roadside limekiln that served them is passed in superb condition. **At the bottom is a barn grouping at Twiston Mill.** Up to a century ago there was a cotton mill here, its waterwheel supplied by the mill dam still to be seen just further along the road.

Pendle Hill from
Skeleron mines

At the driveway, take a wall-stile and turn downstream with Twiston Beck. This delightful section leads through several stiles near the 'twisting' stream to reach a footbridge. Cross and climb the wall-side past a double-trough spring to Springs Farm. What a prospect to savour from your window! Rise up to the buildings and pass the house on the left. Leave the drive at once by a gate on the right, and along the field-side to a stile by a gate. Rise across the field to a prominent wall-stile. Now on a modest ridge-top, head away on a sunken way. When the wall leaves continue with the fence, passing small quarrying scars to reach a wall-stile. Now bear right to Hey House Farm.

Joining its drive 50 yards before the farm, take a prominent wall-stile to neatly avoid the place, and head away with a small wood on the right. Continue on through a couple of intervening stiles, the second in a tiny section of wall. Here there is a choice of finishes. The right of way follows the line of trees left to a stile onto a lane: turn right past an old quarry and limekiln to re-enter Downham. Alternatively, a concessionary path has been created to keep us off the road. Simply continue along the brow of the ridge (the church tower appears ahead) past the cluster of trees, and along to the far end where the outward route is rejoined. From Hey House to this point we have been tracing the line of the Roman road from Ribchester to Elslack. Amid a final scattering of old workings - note the tilted limestone slabs - the outward route leads back down into the village.

Old Well Hall, Downham

AROUND SAWLEY

START Sawley Grid ref. SD 776465

DISTANCE 4 miles

ORDNANCE SURVEY MAPS
1:50,000
Landranger 103 - Blackburn & Burnley
1:25,000
Pathfinder 669 - Clitheroe & Chipping

ACCESS Start from the village centre, by the *Spread Eagle*.
Sawley is served by bus from Clitheroe. There is parking on
the road alongside the river, and also outside the abbey.

THE RIBBLE GORGE

Walk 8 was originally a 6 ½ mile walk entitled *Ribble Gorge*, the
first part of which is a magnificent ramble along the wooded
riverbank above Sawley. Probably the finest section of Ribble-
side walking, it is a major highlight of the popular Ribble Way.
Unfortunately, and unbelievably, it appears that a successful
extinguishment of the public bridleway (coinciding with this
guide's publication) has not at the same time been replaced by
the intended public footpath. As a result of this sudden
development I have been advised not to include the walk.

The many walkers who know Sawley well will be stunned by
this. There may well be some outraged public citizens who
cannot face the potentially long wait for re-instatement of a
public right of way, but that is their decision. Perhaps when you
visit Sawley a public footpath will be open: for my part I will
return *Ribble Gorge* to its rightful place on page 38 at the first
available opportunity. For now I offer this gentler ramble.
Pleasant it is too, but the Ribble Gorge it is not.

Sawley is a lovely Ribble-side village, best known for its monastic remains. Salley (the old name) Abbey was founded by William de Percy for Cistercian monks in 1147. Always in the shadow of nearby Whalley Abbey, it suffered on more than one occasion from marauding Scots. It was also one of the first to suffer at the Dissolution: indeed, its last abbot William Trafford was hanged for his support of the Pilgrimage of Grace. Much of its stone was later removed for building purposes in the district. It is now in the care of English Heritage and open to the public. The fine arched bridge over the river makes a lovely background to the scene presented by the dabbling ducks on the private green by the pub.

☐ **From the corner by the** Spread Eagle **turn along the side road upstream with the Ribble. When it swings away, continue along the drive for Sawley Lodge. On the brow, just past the last buildings, take a bridle-gate on the right and another just above it. This puts us on a firm farm drive. Go left with it, gently rising with a good view of Sawley Lodge down to the left. It rises parallel with a tinkling brook before crossing it. Within fifty yards take a gate on the right, and head up the field-side with the now tiny stream. Beyond a fence-stile in a wall, advance a few yards further then take a stile on the right. Cross the stream and rise to the corrugated barn up to the left. Behind it a rough track leads up to the A59.**

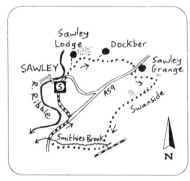

Just across to the right is an Ordnance Survey column, with Longridge Fell directly behind, while Pendle Hill appears ahead. **Cross with care and turn right along a sidelined section of old road, now a popular lay-by. Part-way along take a gate on the left, and double back to a gate midway along a fence on the left. Continue across to another gate into the corner of a field (not the first field behind the farm). Now cross diagonally to a gate in the far corner.**

Over to the left are glimpses of the Ribblesdale pairing of Ingleborough and Penyghent. Ahead, Pendle Hill is truly magnificent now, and will remain so for the whole of this next stage.

Through the gate, turn right with the fence to approach a small plantation. A corner stile sends a slim path straight through, emerging via another stile at the far corner, alongside a little pond. Turn quickly right through a gate and head past the fine barn of Swanside Laithe. Continue again with a fence on the right, all the way along an improving track to the next barn.

From the barn continue down to a gate in the field corner, follow the hedge on the right down to a gate at the bottom corner. Descend the big grassy bank to a bridge on Smithies Brook. This old packhorse bridge is a gem, as is its setting in the charming wooded dean. Rise a few yards then bear right to a tiny footbridge at the far corner. Continue along the wood top to a stile at the end, then a path slants down to the brook. Follow it closely downstream to Smithies Bridge on the A59. Cross and turn right, tramping the verge as far as the Sawley turning, then go down the road to finish. Passing through the village, features of interest include a 1720 datestone on a cottage opposite the phone box: alongside this the now abandoned old road rises away. Further on is the old village school of 1876, and then the abbey itself is reached.

Packhorse bridge,
Smithies Brook

GRINDLETON FELL

START Grindleton   Grid ref. SD 758454

DISTANCE 5¼ miles

ORDNANCE SURVEY MAPS
1:50,000
Landranger 103 - Blackburn & Burnley
1:25,000
Pathfinder 669 - Clitheroe & Chipping

ACCESS The walk begins from the sloping main street. Grindleton is served by bus from Clitheroe. Parking is somewhat limited: there is a layby at the top of the village, past all the houses by a Forest of Bowland sign.

☐ *Climb to the top of the main street and out of the village past the parking area. Just short of the three-storeyed house at Steelands take a gate at a footpath sign on the left. Descend towards a footbridge over a tree-lined beck. Without crossing the bridge, turn upstream a few yards and secure a crossing through undergrowth and branches. Head straight up the field behind, alongside a smaller tree-lined tributary. Keep going all the way to a wall along the top. From the stile by the gate turn left with the wall, running along the side to approach the buildings at Cob House.*

Joining the top of its drive, turn immediately right through a gate, from where a welcoming green way rises. Longridge Fell is seen way over to the left. At the end the way emerges into a field, and here take a stile on the left. A rusting sign (the first of several along the route) proclaims this as Clitheroe Corporation's old gathering grounds. Descend a wall-side, soon transferring at a stile to follow a fence down to a hidden footbridge in the corner. Cross to the ruins of Simpshey, taking a slanting trod up behind to the start of an old walled way in the corner above. Go left on it, soon opening out and curving up to the right.

By the time the brow is reached the track has completely faded. From a forlorn gatepost cross to the sturdy wall corner on the right, and follow the wall away to a waiting green lane. This aims directly for the dark cloak of Grindleton Forest to join a stony lane. Cross over and go through the gatepost just to the left, to find a superb path rising through the trees, courtesy of Forest Enterprise. Non-claustrophobic, it climbs delightfully through twin gateposts to arrive at the ruin of Mount Pleasant. Here a forest road is met. Turn right on it, crossing a tiny beck at some pheasant pens. Here leave the track, and bear right on the crumbling wall-side rising through a break. Through heather and bracken a thin path shadows the wall, soon running along the level to quickly reach a crossroads with a firmer track (the public footpath) at a wall junction. Here turn right, descending to reach the terminus of a hard forest road alongside a vast felled area on the left.

Almost at once this is left by a clear footpath opposite, through a reedy corner and running on the short way to the end of a wall. Here turn left on the far side of the wall (waymarked), and a good path curves around the trees. The wall is replaced by a fence, and soon the path runs on to enter a superb green lane outside the trees. This is Shivering Ginnel, which climbs away between field and forest. At a corner take a stile on the left to leave the trees behind. Winding up again, the way remains a gem until ending abruptly and out of character in a muddy gateway. The path continues with the left-hand wall, its sunken course unmistakable.

However, the Ordnance column (S5159) atop Beacon Hill, just to the right, beckons. A stunning panorama is revealed, with Pendle Hill, Ribble Valley, South and West Pennines to east and south. The view north draws most eyes, a stunning prospect of the peaks of the southern Yorkshire Dales, with the shapely duo of Ingleborough and Penyghent the magnets. The former, in particular, seems especially detached, isolated and majestic, while the Wharfedale giants of Buckden Pike and Great Whernside also feature.

Returning to the wall, head off again to a corner stile. The line remain true, a sunken old way runs a bee-line to a gate onto a lane. Go right, descending just as far as Scriddles Farm. Take a gate opposite it and descend a field-side to find a corner stile onto a narrow lane at white-walled Rod Hill House. Go left to its terminus at Till House, or more correctly, the house down below it. The line of the path is currently subject of a local dispute, but the present waymark leads into the front garden and along to a gate: if a change is waymarked, it will go round the back of the house.

Slant down to a stile in the corner of the paddock and down the field-side to enter a much larger field. From the bottom corner head down the next field to a footbridge. Across, forsake the natural line up the pasture, and take a stile on the left. Climb the centre of the field to two trees skyline trees. Sawley is now in view below. Turn sharp right on the brow to the nearest fence corner, just past which is a gate. Go left with the fence to the farm buildings at Hill House.

Entering the yard pass the modern barns, go left at the first chance to the main farmyard, then right past the house to a gate into a field. Advance with the fence to the end. Pendle Hill is yet again mightily impressive over to the left. Take the central gate into a field corner, and follow the natural line up the hedge-side on the right. A part sunken way mounts the gentle brow, and this same way leads unerringly back to Grindleton, initially along a broad ridge. This smashing old way known as High Chapel Lane takes a variety of guises, but the near straight line remains clear all the way to becoming encased in a tunnel of foliage (at the start of this, ignore a stile on the left). This splendid final section leads into a private looking yard. Keep right to emerge back onto the main street.

Bowland from Beacon Hill

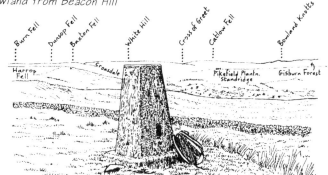

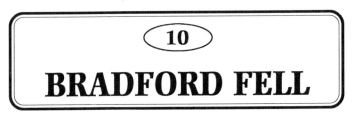

10

BRADFORD FELL

START West Bradford   Grid ref. SD 742443

DISTANCE 6 or 8¼ miles

ORDNANCE SURVEY MAPS
1:50,000
Landranger 103 - Blackburn & Burnley
1:25,000
Pathfinder 669 - Clitheroe & Chipping

ACCESS Start from the village centre. West Bradford is served by bus from Clitheroe. There is limited parking on wider sections of the main street, and a parking area on the Clitheroe side of Bradford Bridge (GR 745439). The *Three Millstones* has a car park, so genuine patrons might earn a place there by asking nicely. A more eccentric starting point is the high point of the walk, on the summit of the Waddington-Slaidburn road - this way, there's a pub half-way round!

This lengthy expedition climbs - potentially from the Ribble's bank - over 1000ft to the crest of the broad fell dividing Ribble and Hodder. The outer and return routes are never little more than half a mile apart, and even merge for a short section on the higher ground. The contrasting terrain is just one fine aspect of the walk as we rise from pastures to felltop: views too, are outstanding, though it is the surround of colourful fell country that will be remembered. Incidentally, those armed with the sister guidebook to BOWLAND might consider walking into real Bowland by descending the other side of the fell to Slaidburn: check the bus times.

☐ *West Bradford is an unassuming village which lets neighbouring Waddington grab the plaudits. Pub, Post office and church all play their part in maintaining a community atmosphere. Note the old pinfold on the right near the top of the main street.* **At the head of the main street turn left on the Waddington road.** *At once note the* *fine old house of Pillings just up to the right, with its mullioned windows.* **Head past the** Three Millstones **and rising above the beck, turn up the lane towards Eaves Hall. An early flight of steps on the left leads into a field. Head away with the fence to an old iron kissing-gate, and advance to cross a side-stream by a tiny footbridge.** *Back over to the right is a glimpse of the grandiose red brick facade of Eaves Hall (1922), now a country club. High above is the TV mast on Waddington Fell, for which we're aiming.*

Follow another fence away to a stile, then take a wooden kissing-gate on the right. Go left to a fence, and follow it up the field to reach the buildings above. Go through a gate at the top, outside the garden of the first house to join its drive. Cross straight over into a field, up the side of the second, and then across to a gate in the wall behind it. Head straight up the next two fields to the houses at Dove Sike, above. A stile leads to a short enclosed way between them. On the drive, turn right.

Easington Fell

Walloper Well

quarry

Bradford Fell

Waddington Fell

B6478

Grindleton Forest

N

Seedalls   Hancocks   Brocklehurst

Dove Sike

S

WEST BRADFORD

River Ribble

Quickly joined by another track, take the stile on the left and slant up to the top of a line of trees. From a stile and slab bridge resume the slant towards the farmhouse at Hancocks. Here Moor Lane, still surfaced, is rejoined and followed uphill, resplendent in hollies. Soon it terminates by bearing off to Seedalls Farm. We advance straight up to a gate into the corner of a pasture. From this reedy corner a good path follows the fence up. Far over to the right, Grindleton Forest sprawls. Behind us, Pendle is currently marred by the cement works. **Beyond a barn, Moor Lane settles down into a part enclosed green track, ever gently gaining height.** A stage is quickly reached where we are entirely surrounded by real fell country: heather moor, bracken and moor grass forging a colourful combination. **Mostly in good shape, the track rises to a distinct** *corner beyond a gate. Yards further, it swings right along a line of poor shooting hides, and maintains this Roman-like march past a reed-fringed pool along to a T-junction with another such lane.*

This is the point to which we shall return, so anyone flagging can sit down and wait for the fitter members of the party. **Turn up the green lane to soon reach a corner. The main track bears left, while a branch diverts up to the prominent cairn above before working back to it at the far corner. Here, by a pair of forlorn gateposts, we shall return after a loop of the felltop and a visit to Walloper Well.** Here too, the Bowland skyline appears ahead, ranging from Parlick in the south to White Hill in the north. **The more obvious way heading off is our return path, so for now, take the initially less obvious and less appealing track bearing off to the left, aiming directly for the mast on Waddington Fell.** This great mass of fell has any number of names appended to it, depending on which part you're on at the time. Though Waddington Fell is perhaps the most widely used, Easington, Newton, Harrop, Grindleton and Bradford also stake their claims, and for us the latter is most appropriate.

The track quickly becomes clearer as it runs along the moor, on to a gateway and along to join the road summit at the entrance to Waddington Fell Quarries. Turn right, over the cattle-grid to the parking area, and head off along the verge. The road begins to descend, but we go only as far as Walloper Well. Here spring water pours into the roadside troughs. **Now it's back onto the moor: turn down to cross the grassy retaining wall of an old dam.** This drained

reservoir served a waterwheel that worked a small lead smelting mill downstream. **Rise up beyond it to a shooting butt, just past which is a splendid green, part-sunken track. Turn right, and at a major fork keep right. This runs back across the moor, passing near a prominent cairn.** This is known as the Wife, presumably the spuse of Old Ned, another nearby cairn. **Beyond an iron ladder-stile over the wall, the path rejoins the outward route at the gateposts. Bowland is replaced by Pendle: retrace steps back to the corner and down to the T-junction.**

Walloper Well

46

This time continue straight down the green lane outside Grindleton Forest. A forest road soon comes in to replace the pleasant surface. *Ahead, Pendle looks more comfortable having distanced itself somewhat from the cement works.* Continue a short way further down, then just above the long ruined farm of St. Clares, go through a gap in the wall and head away on a distinct green track. Beyond a beck crossing take a stile in a fence midway between the corner and a gate ahead. Now follow a long crumbled wall across to the shell of the more recently abandoned Fell Side.

On its other side a green way heads down between walls. From the gate at the end it becomes unclear. Advance a short way with the wall, from where the track resurrects itself as a reedy line to perform a big dog-leg down this steeper pasture. From a gate in the bottom corner go straight down the reedy line towards a side-stream. Cross beneath a marshy confluence, and breast the slope behind to a gate where wall and fence meet. Head away with a wall, and a fine green track quickly forms to lead down through the fields onto a surfaced drive.

Continue down to the lane-side farm at Brocklehurst. Just beyond, take a gate on the right into a large field just past the head of a wooded beck. Head away, keeping a distance from the trees to reach a stream crossing. Now slant off to the left, descending to a gate with adjacent stile. *The rooftops of West Bradford now appear below.* Slant down again, passing above a hedge corner, on line for Clitheroe Castle, straight ahead. Go down through a scant line of hawthorns, and down to join the foot of a drive just above a farm. This leads through the yard and out onto the road at the head of the village.

The Three Millstones, *West Bradford*

11

WADDINGTON

START   Bradford Bridge   Grid ref. SD 745439

DISTANCE   7 ¾ miles

ORDNANCE SURVEY MAPS
1:50,000
Landranger 103 - Blackburn & Burnley
1:25,000
Pathfinder 669 - Clitheroe & Chipping

ACCESS   Start from the small car park on the Clitheroe side
of the bridge. There is also some roadside parking. Clitheroe-
West Bradford buses run past. An alternative start is
Waddington itself, also served by Clitheroe buses.

☐ *Cross the bridge and head along the lane towards the village.
As the road turns away take a stile to stay with the river, through
the bottom of a garden and over a footbridge to gain the bank
proper. A lovely riverbank walk ensues, first enclosed then through
a broad pasture before being deflected by fence and side-stream.
Beyond a stile this leads to a sewage works. From its bridge regain
the riverbank to resume upstream. With unglamorous Grindleton
Bridge in view ahead, the path swings left to a stile to rise as a
snicket past the former Riverside Mill onto the West Bradford road.*

*Turn right and follow the road as it swings up towards the village.
Both the Duke of York and the Buck Inn are set around a junction:
here turn left to climb the main street proper. This lengthy pull is
punctuated by noticing some attractive corners. On reaching the
bus turning area at Top of Town, turn left through a farmyard
directly opposite. Go straight ahead to a gate into the field, and
descend to find a footbridge on Grindleton Brook. A path slants up
the other side, and follows the tree-lined side-stream away. From
a stile at the end, continue along a couple more field-sides to
emerge onto Green Lane, which lives up to its name.*

Turn up Green Lane, its condition improving to rise alongside a wood, where it becomes firmer before reaching the farm buildings at White Hall. Where the drive to Far House turns off to the left, leave also, but not up the drive. Instead, enter the field and double back left between the track we've left and the farm drive. This large pasture is crossed wth an intervening stile as guide, gradually crossing to the edge of a drop to West Clough Brook. At the far corner a faint green track is joined. Go left through the gate and on to a footbridge behind, then slant up the brow. Cross the field-side to a waterworks building at Lowcocks. Go round to the right of the farm buildings behind, and follow the drive out to a junction.

Go left just as far as the first bend, where a ladder-stile admits to the field on the right. Now head away along the field tops. Pendle Hill is resplendant from here, display-ing its full length over to the left. A stile on the right is reached just short of the woods ahead. *Now a track leads down to cross Drakehouse Brook, climbing back out of the wooded environs to reach Drake House. This is a busy spot with kennels and stables. While*

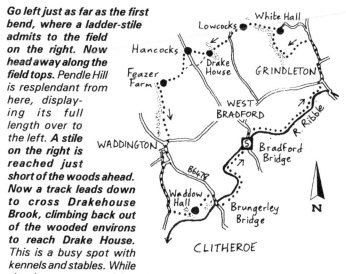

the dogs may sound ferocious, they just want to join your walk: don't let them! *As the drive heads away, take a gate on the right and slant up to the far corner. Two stiles in succession point the way to cross a field to the farm buildings at Hancocks. A gate near the right end admits to the yard: go first right, next left, then through a private looking gate to emerge onto surfaced Moor Lane.*

Cross straight over to a gate, and slant across to the bottom corner of the field, doing likewise in the next one. This admits to a drive. Turn right as it runs along to Dove Sike. Keep right of both houses, and from the gate there bear right to cross a marshy stream. Behind, rise to a gateway and cross a field top to the buildings at

49

Feazer Farm. Take a gate to the right of a bungalow and follow the drive away past the farm. As it swings right, a path delves left towards the trees to find a sturdy stile in the wall corner. Now simply head down the long, narrow field outside the wooded gill.

At the second fence, with Waddington in view ahead huddled round its church tower, we are deflected in a more direct line away from the wood, down to a corner stile. Continue down from it along a line of trees to find the field narrowing before emptying us onto a road in Waddington. Turn right for the village centre. *Passed on the way are the almshouses originally endowed in 1700 by one of the long established Parker family of nearby Browsholme Hall. In more recent times they have been rebuilt in this lovely setting.*

Picturesque Waddington has long been a showpiece village. Waddington Brook tinkles through the length of the village - eclipsing the good efforts of West Bradford's stream - and proves the focal point of this cosy community. Floral displays, stone cottages and the church all combine to form a grand scene. There are two pubs, a tearoom and a Post office/store. St. Helen's church was largely rebuilt in 1901, but retains its solid buttressed tower of 1501. Inside one finds a 15th century font and some medieval glass. Though restored a century ago, much of the old hall dates back over 500 years: Henry VI spent a year or so here after defeat at Hexham in 1464 during the Wars of the Roses.

Leave the main street just below the war memorial, where stepping stones cross the brook and a field-path heads away to join a lane. *Just up to the right is the welcoming* Buck Inn. *More commonly referred to as the* Lower Buck *- to distinguish it from the other 'Buck' - this superb country inn dates back around 300 years.* **Head left along the lane, going left at a junction and then keeping straight on past a turning for Clitheroe. Another little stream runs another parallel course before we leave the last of the houses for a half-mile along the quiet back lane. On a bend, a footpath sign sends us through a gate on the left, where the back drive to Waddow Hall runs through parkland beneath a limestone knoll.**

We are deflected up behind the house, returning at the other side to join its main drive. *The hall dates back to Tudor times, but has been substantially enlarged since then: for many years now it has been used as a girl guide centre.* **Its drive heads away, ignoring an early left branch.** *Ahead, the proximity of the cement works impinges surprisingly little on our Pendle horizons.* **At a fork with**

the road and the Ribble in sight, the old drive bears off to the right to emerge via a stile onto the Waddington road. Go right to descend to cross Brungerley Bridge. Built in the early 19th century, it is inscribed with both townships and (real) counties it divides: 'Clitheroe, Lancashire; Waddington, Yorkshire'.

A short distance along the other side an urban path heads off to the left, past some well camouflaged toilets. This area is a public park, entirely wooded and very pleasant. *Our route avoids all branch paths by remaining on that nearest the river. A short way along, a few yards' diversion leads to a carved sculpture on the bank.* Labelled 'Saving Sheep', by Thompson Dagnall, it was carved from local dead elms. It is the principle feature of the Ribble Valley Sculpture Trail created in 1993, and portrays a shepherd's fight to save a straying sheep from the swelling river's current. **Continue upstream past an abundance of seats, noting a branch off to an old quarry. Just past this the path forks, and our riverside branch drops down to quickly leave the trees. Clinging tightly to the bank around a large bend, we shortly arrive back at the three arches of Bradford Bridge.**

By the Ribble:
'Saving Sheep' and Bradford Bridge

51

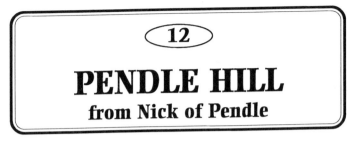

PENDLE HILL
from Nick of Pendle

START Nick of Pendle   Grid ref. SD 771385

DISTANCE 6½ miles

ORDNANCE SURVEY MAPS
1:50,000
Landranger 103 - Blackburn & Burnley
1:25,000
Pathfinder 680 - Longridge & Great Harwood
Outdoor Leisure 21 - South Pennines (1995 edition) replaces
Pathfinders 669 and 670 *or*
Paths around Pendle footpath map covers the whole route

ACCESS Start from a sizeable parking area on the crest of the road (Sabden side). Sabden is served by Burnley/Padiham-Whalley/Clitheroe buses.

Apart from the first and last miles, this walk is not on public rights of way, but on concessionary paths: please respect these routes.

☐ **From the parking area cross to the broad track opposite. This heads off firmly and decisively along the crest of the broad ridge.** *With no navigational problems and superb views from the outset, just stride out! Clitheroe and the Ribble Valley feature to the left, and beyond is Longridge Fell and a Bowland skyline. Prominent early on are the Deerstones over to the right (see WALK 13). This track over the moor links ancient Bronze age sites, one being the large pile of stones passed on Apronfull Hill. Down to the right is Churn Clough Reservoir.*

A green track branches off for Deerstones, while our way forges on up the slopes. A pile of stones on a brow signals the revelation of Pendle's great expanse, vast moorland slopes culminating in the broad summit - no inclination of Pendle's familiar Big End outline here! **At a major brow in the saddle linking with Spence Moor to the right, Ogden Clough is seen taking shape ahead, a fine foreground to the great dome of the summit area behind. As the track turns upstream with it, there are fine views back down the steep walled clough.**

Approaching a crumbling wall, transfer to a path that has developed on the right, to run along the inside of the clough. This is a superb stage, a grand path running through the clough, with the stream tumbling over stony ledges below: classic Pennine stuff. **In time the clough eases and path and brook come together.** Here, on the right, note the free-standing boundary stone inscribed 'WA'. This grassy bank is a grand place to linger; not only in its own right, but because beyond here are several exposed miles, beginning with a peaty climb.

Downham Moor

Mearley Clough

∏ 1828'

Pendle Hill

Ashendean Clough

Ogden Clough

Spence Moor

Wellsprings Inn

Nick of Pendle

N

Just yards beyond the stone, with a wall in view ahead, the path crosses the brook to a cairn and climbs away through eroded peat groughs. Looking back, there is nothing but moorland, yet we are nearing civilisation all the time, in the form of the escape route down to Barley. **The gradient quickly eases but the peat relents less readily. Only as the Ordnance column (S2161) on Pendle's summit appears does the terrain improve, finishing over bare stony turf.**

Arrival on a summit is always a good moment, and here we have the added bonus of the hitherto unseen view eastwards. There can be no day of the year when no-one ventures up, and the likelihood is that there will be many folk here, for almost everyone uses the Barley 'tourist' path, usually both up and down. First reward is a perch on the rim of the mighty drop, enjoying a bird's-eye view over Barley as it nestles in its fold of the hills. Pendle's isolation ensures extensive views in all directions, with the South and West Pennine moors beyond the East Lancashire conurbations, and a long Dales line-up to the north. Bowland, to the west, is merely a skyline, but reveals itself on the return leg. Note that if time be pressing or visibility poor, then one might wish to return by the route of ascent.

Leave by following the path heading north to a gate and ladder-stile in the sturdy wall (or perhaps tramp the edge while you can). Cross the stile and bear gently left away from the wall, on a superb green pathway that heads north-west to the high point of Downham Moor. This is a classic stride with the view to match, ahead to the Bowland skyline and north to the Dales peaks. **Approaching a wall again (the one rising from the head of the clough) the path bears right to another prominent ladder-stile.**

Fifty yards to the left a boundary stone encased in the wall is inscribed 'D', with benchmark; and 'W' on the other side: these refer to Downham and Worston. A far more significant development is the wondrous prospect now on display, over the steep flanks to the Bowland moors across the Ribble Valley. Countless villages are laid out as on a map: see WALK 6 for more on this classic view.

Over the stile, another boundary stone (inscribed 'W') stands alone down to the right. **On contrastingly bare, short turf head along the scarp to the monster shelter.** Solidly built as recently as 1983, it is well furnished with seating. It is also well appreciated on the right kind of day, of which Pendle has many! **Resume along the edge to the next objective, the major landmark of the Scout Cairn.** This proves to be a well constructed 10ft pillar, a well known Ribble Valley landmark. Memorial tablets set into it explain its name.

The shelter on the western edge, looking to Longridge Fell

Further significance is accorded to the Scout Cairn as it is also an important route marker. This is the point to which the Downham route, used in WALK 6, gains the edge. Here a commonly used route back towards the Nick forges on around the head of Mearley Clough on the less well defined, initially peaty edge. Although this direct return to the Wellsprings Inn by way of the wall and Ashendean Clough is a popular route in regular use, and featured in other guides, the landowners, upon consultation, are not keen to have it publicised. **As a result, guidance in this book is to turn south-east from the vicinity of the Scout Cairn, crossing a short stretch of open moor on the largely undefined estate boundary to drop down into upper Ogden Clough. Here the outward route is rejoined, and steps can be retraced back to the Nick.**

If refreshment is sought, a variation can be made near the end to incorporate the Wellsprings Inn, **by curving down a wide, hollowed grassy way onto the road.** One might also watch the antics of those on the dry ski slope of the Pendle Ski Club. **The Nick of Pendle is now just a few minutes up the road, but as it can be quite busy, one can always shun the tarmac by turning back up the hollowed way. At the top, the start is just along to the right.**

The Scout Cairn, looking north to the shelter

SPENCE MOOR

START Sabden   Grid ref. SD 779374

DISTANCE 5½ miles

ORDNANCE SURVEY MAPS
1:50,000
Landranger 103 - Blackburn & Burnley
1:25,000
Pathfinder 680 - Longridge & Great Harwood
681 - Burnley *or* Outdoor Leisure 21 (1995 edition) *or*
Paths around Pendle footpath map covers the whole route

ACCESS Start from the village centre. there is a car park opposite the *White Hart*. Sabden is served by Burnley/Padiham-Whalley/Clitheroe buses. An alternative start is the large car park on Padiham Heights, due south of the village.

There is a lot more to the Pendle massif than the casual visitor appreciates, and this walk proves a good example. Sabden is an industrialised village, home of the once secretive treacle mines to which visitors are now admitted. Not forgetting the better known side of the area, there is also a Pendle Witch *pub just round the corner, and an antiques centre.*

☐ *From the crossroads in the village centre, turn right along Wesley Street, bound for St. Nicholas' church, Heyhouses.* Dating from 1846, its thin west tower tapers to a spire. *Before reaching it turn left along the lane for Badger Wells Cottages. This rises to a junction at Cockshotts Farm. Go left over the beck and up to the front of the terrace. Pass to the right of it, where a path heads into the trees behind, alongside a wall. Emerging through a gate at the top, the next stages of the walk appear.* High above, beyond the attractive Churn Clough, the Deerstones on Spence Moor break the skyline. Look back also, over the church spire to Padiham Heights. *Head straight up the inviting pasture, turning through a kissing-gate at the top corner and resuming alongside a small side-beck. Grand strides lead up to a kissing-gate onto the foot of the moor.*

The path rises a little further to meet a broad track. Turn right along this cart-track, passing briefly through the top of a field before rejoining the moor. It runs on in lovely surroundings to cross a stream in tree-lined surrounds. Winding round the bank opposite it runs on again, now as a path, to the corner of a larch plantation. On crossing another side-stream, the path rises up with it, soon leaving the trees behind.

*Climbing through the bracken with the Deerstones ahead, keep left at a fork, crossing a tiny stream with the steep-sided clough on the left. The path quickly shrugs off the bracken and scales the broad shoulder falling from the Deerstones. As the edge is gained, a fine prospect opens out westwards to Longridge Fell and the southern Bowland moors. **The path now scales the modest edge, crossing over a green trackway and quickly reaching the highest point of the edge.** The few modest outcrops at the Deerstones overlook a deep, boulder-filled amphitheatre.*

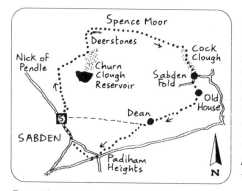

Resume the walk by doubling back to join the wall over to the left, perhaps making use of the grassy track passed earlier. Don't be tempted by the ladder-stile there, but simply follow the wall-side path eastwards to another prominent ladder-stile.

*From the stile a path heads directly away across Spence Moor, initially rather moist. It soon picks up, and enjoys a fine march. On the brow the summit of the moor, and the walk, is reached at 1509ft. Ahead, the great prow of Pendle looms across to our left beyond the hidden ravine of Ogden Clough. The extensive panorama features Burn Moor, Barden Moor, Skipton Moor, Earl Crag, Boulsworth Hill and all along the South and West Pennine moors back to Longridge Fell and Bowland. **The path begins its descent by angling down to the wall, where a ladder-stile awaits. From its descend the poorest part of the walk, keeping left of a reedy line alongside a long crumbled wall. There is no complete escape from the mire here. From a stile by a gate at the bottom, relief is*** *immediate. Turn down the wall-side above a deep little ravine to a gateway at the bottom beneath the vestiges of an old barn. Head down the wall-side outside the head of wooded Cock Clough.*

When a fence takes over look out for a stile in it to gain access to the woods. Turn down the clough, remaining inside the wall until it turns away. Here go straight down the tongue in front, a path appearing at the end to lead down to a small confluence. Cross the left-hand stream and resume on a clearer path to the bottom of the wood. With a scruffy open area just behind the farm ahead, look back to appreciate a couple of lovely waterslides. A vague path doubles back down to the stream, crossing beneath another hitherto unseen waterfall, and back out the other side above a couple of little dams. Just below is a fence-stile, from where continue down the grassy bank opposite the farm and its main pond. Just below, emerge onto a lane adjacent to the farm.

Turn right down this lane as far as a sharp bend. Here continue straght down the drive to the Old House. Go straight ahead to the

gate right of the house, and down an enclosure towards the confluence of two meandering streams, a lovely spot. Take the little bridge over the right-hand one, and a little further downstream is a stile in a short section of wall. From it bear away from the stream, rounding a gentle brow to locate a stile in the fence opposite. Turn right to a stile at the end of the field. Head away with the fence, and when it turns off go straight ahead towards the abandoned farmhouse at Drivers.

Deerstones,
Spence Moor

Go round the back, and turn down a track towards the bottom corner. Don't use the stile there but turn right on a green track along the bottom of the field. *Below is the chirpy Sabden Brook, which quickly performs an impressive, wispish ox-bow routine before it heads away.* **We keep straight on to the prominent gap-stile by the gate ahead.** *Across to our left throughout this is the long, ridge of Pendle Forest. It screens the bustling East Lancashire world beyond, though not the drone of motorway traffic. Over to the right now are the slopes of Spence Moor.* **From the stile steps are drawn to the far corner of the field on a forming track bound for Dean Farm. From the corner stile the track runs along to the farm. A kissing-gate to the left admits to the head of the drive. Follow it round to the left of the house and out.** *On drawing level with the house, a surprise awaits as the hitherto normal house reveals its other side - a superb old frontage sporting mullioned windows and a carved inscription.*

Resuming, the drive leads all the way to Sabden. A more interesting, relatively effortless finish, however, turns off at a new footbridge. Crossing Sabden Brook, bear right up the field to the start of a wall. Pass to its right, and as it turns away keep straight on to slant across to a stile in the wall ahead. This admits to the rough pasture slopes of the Height. Turn right on a thin path that rises imperceptibly away from the fence to reach a stile in the wall ahead. Continue across this more inviting pasture to the lone oak tree at the wall corner ahead, and continue with the wall.

At the next corner is a crossroads of green ways. Advance a few yards then slant up the inviting grassy rake. *Super views over the hidden valley of Pendle Forest include most of our walk, dominated by Spence Moor's bracken flanks.* **The old way leads up to a stile in a wall corner, behind which is a crossroads on Padiham Heights. Bear right along the ridge-top road past the car park. A little further, take a stile on the right and follow the fence to a corner. With Sabden outspread below, the path slants down the colourful flank bound for the village. It leads all the way down to the bottom corner, where a stile admits onto the road on the very edge of the village. Turn down the road to finish.**

59

(14)

ROUGHLEE

START Barrowford   Grid ref. SD 862397

DISTANCE 5 ½ miles

ORDNANCE SURVEY MAPS
1:50,000
Landranger 103 - Blackburn & Burnley
1:25,000
Outdoor Leisure 21 - South Pennines (1995 edition) replaces
Pathfinders 670 and 681

ACCESS Start from Pendle Heritage Centre at the top end
of the village. There is a car park across the road (donations
please), and further parking around the main street. Barrowford
can be reached from Colne, Nelson and Burnley by bus.

*Pendle Heritage Centre is run by the Lancashire Heritage Trust,
based in the splendid old house of Park Hill. It is open daily
(admission fee to main features, including an exhibition on the
Story of Pendle, and the Pendle Witches) and has a shop and
tearoom. Also on view is a 14th century cruck barn, a display of
farm tools, and 18th century walled gardens. Park Hill dates from
the 17th century, and was home to generations of the Bannisters.
Purchased by the local council in 1920, it was restored in more
recent times. The Pendle Way was opened here in 1987. Over the
bridge is the toll house built in 1805 to serve the Nelson (then
Marsden)-Long Preston turnpike: purchased by the trust in 1983,
restoration included the old toll board.*

❑ *From the centre a path runs down through the public park,
alongside the beck to a footbridge. Across the road is the attractive
front of the* White Bear *inn, dating from the 17th century: note the
three-storeyed porch and mullioned windows.* **Cross the bridge and
the road and go up the side of the inn, continuing up past most of
the housing to a sharp bend. Here go straight ahead on the Pasture**

*House farm drive alongside a white house. Over to the right, Stansfield Tower on Blacko Hill is prominent. **Half-way up, beyond the allotments, look for a stile on the left as a path heads along a hedge-side. Turn right at the first opportunity, rising by a line of hollies to become enclosed by hollies. At the top, pass alongside a barn and up the next field, now with a line of trees on the left.***

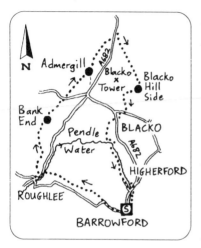

*A pronounced brow is quickly reached. Here is a magnificent prospect, with Pendle Hill dominating all, including its underlings Spence Moor and Burn Moor. **Down below our first objective, Roughlee, reveals itself on reaching a stile at the end, as stone walls replace foliage.** While its caravan sites are most prominent, the old hall can also be discerned. **Head down the field, slanting left at the bottom to the sturdy cylindrical stepping stones on Pendle Water. Behind, the road is joined.***

*A direct route is up the farm drive opposite, but Roughlee merits a detour left. By the bridge stands the Bay Horse, with a children's playground. Return along the front of a row of white cottages, immediately off the junction just short of the pub. **This narrows to run along the front of Roughlee Old Hall.** This superb old house with mullioned windows - some arch-headed - bears a weathered 1536 datestone from an earlier building. It was reputedly home of Alice Nutter, the one 'lady' among the clutch of Pendle Witches.*

Turn up the drive at the end, passing through Hollin Farm and on to the house at Middlewood. Through the gate at the end advance along the field-side, using where possible an old way overgrown with hollies. Just short of the end cross to a gate over to the left. Slant right to follow the wall up, using a stile midway to trace its other side to a stile into attractive Bank End Wood. Rising up, a thin path quickly swings right, rising gradually to the far end. Approaching the house at Bank End, take a slimmer branch up to the left to a stile in the wall corner. Cross the field bottom above the house and keep straight on through a new plantation.

61

With the drive just over the wall, don't join it but keep straight on to a stile in the facing wall, a little left of the corner. Head down another area of scattered young plantings, bearing slightly left to drop down to a stile at the bottom. Cross a side-stream and with the main beck over to the right, head straight up the field to find a stile opposite, beneath a telegraph pole. With another stile to the right, slant across the field to join the road via stone steps at a red brick bridge. Cross the road, not the bridge, and descend steps to a slab bridge at a confluence. Over the side-stream, follow Admergill Water upstream on a slim green path.

Through several pastures we reach the hamlet at Lower Admergill, just beyond a footbridge. A stile leads into the garden of the nearest house. Go right out on the drive, and right over a cattle-grid and bridge. At the first bend, take the drive along to the left to Admergill Hall Farm. On crossing the beck note the old slab bridge: a deep groove worn in the centre suggests regular usage in packhorse days. The hall is a splendid early 17th century house, with leaning mullioned windows, some arch-headed. *Keep straight on the drive until it turns up to the left by a seat.* Burn Moor rises high above. *Keep straight on upstream, through pleasant pasture with wildlife ponds, to arrive at two stiles.* That on the left gives access to Countryside Stewardship land, a bracken-clad patch where visitors are welcome to potter. This is home to upland ground nesting birds such as snipe and curlew, and a breeding ground for brown hares. Admergill Hall Farm is a proud winner of a trophy for the best managed part-time farm in Lancashire, 1993.

Pendle from above Roughlee

62

Roughlee Old Hall

Take the right-hand stile, cross a slab bridge and climb steeply up the bank, bound for the gate on the skyline. *Super views over the upper reaches of this side valley are enjoyed.* **Near the top the thin path slants across to the gate, using a stile to emerge onto the A682.** *Just along to the left is the* Moorcock Inn. **From the stile opposite, however, a path slants up to a wall corner with a farm behind. Here leave the Pendle Way, by doubling back right along the wall-side.** *Over to the right, Pendle is fully revealed again.* **At the end, slant across the large field well above a bield.** *Sat in the field centre, this is a good example of a sheep shelter.*

A sturdy stile in the opposite wall will not be located until upon it, whence cross the flat pasture to the far corner. *Stansfield Tower on Blacko Hill, built around 1890, is now at its nearest point, just over to the right. Access is by permission from Tower Farm. Down to the left the Foulridge Reservoirs appear, backed by Kelbrook Moor.* **From a stile in the rounded corner, continue away to the right with a line of hawthorns, descending the field-side to the farm at Blacko Hill Side. Pass between the buildings and then right, along the front of the house and out on the drive.** *Up to the right, the tower still broods over us.* **The drive turns to descend by a line of hollies to emerge alongside some modern housing onto the road at Blacko.**

Stansfield Tower: Pendle behind

63

Turn right for 100 yards, then left down a modern cul-de-sac, Malkin Close. A footpath slopes off to the right to emerge between houses onto the A682. Cross to a gap-stile almost opposite, then over the field to the corner gateway. Continue away with the fence, but when it parts company, bear left with a line of trees to shadow the wooded gill down to a stile. Descend further with the tiny stream to approach Water Meetings. *Just a minute or so on the path upstream, Blacko Water merges into Pendle Water. In simpler days past this was a popular local stroll and picnic spot.*

Cross the footbridge and turn downstream for a grand walk to Higherford. *En route, an old weir still makes a splash: note also isolated Old Oak Tree Cottage.* **At the end, look back for a final glimpse of the tumbling beck before running along to join the residential Barleydale Road. Keep on to reach the old bridge just round the corner.** *Higherford Bridge dates originally from packhorse times.* **Cross the bridge to Pinfold and onto the main road. Cross the road and turn right past the Old Bridge Inn.** *An old window proclaims the virtues of 'Hartley & Bell's Noted Ales', from a long defunct local brewery.* **Don't cross the modern bridge at this busy corner: for the last lap, turn down a path to the wooded bank of the beck, which is traced downstream to the start.**

Park Hill, Barrowford - the Pendle Heritage Centre

15

GREAT MITTON

START   Clitheroe   Grid ref. SD 726414

DISTANCE   4 ¼ miles

ORDNANCE SURVEY MAPS
1:50,000
Landranger 103 - Blackburn & Burnley
1:25,000
Pathfinder 669 - Clitheroe & Chipping
             680 - Longridge & Great Harwood

ACCESS   Start from Edisford Bridge, a mile out of town on the B6243. There is a large car park just before it.

Edisford (older name Eadsford) Bridge was the scene of a skirmish in 1138 between Scots and Normans. Prior to the ancient bridge, a ford existed here on the Clitheroe-Lancaster medieval way.

☐ **From the car park return to the road where a path runs down to the riverside and the bridge. Cross the bridge and turn immediately down the open bank.** *This opening section, all the way to the waterworks building mentioned below, is a concessionary path courtesy of the landowner.* **Just short of the end of the area, take a stile on the right and follow the hedge away. Towards the corner, slant up to find a stile in the top corner.**

Look back to see Pendle Hill rising beyond Clitheroe. **Behind the stile is a second, from where a track heads into the woods. Emerging at the other end, join the riverbank and follow the Ribble downstream through a sweeping pasture. At the end a stile enters more natural woodland, and a grand little path climbs the bank.**

A stile empties into a field. *Ahead is the outline of Longridge Fell.* **Cross to the right of the waterworks building ahead, past which either of two stiles admit to a small enclosure. Take a gate at the end to reach a junction of ways. To the right, a track comes down from the road, while our way takes the stile ahead, to the left. From**

it head left along the field-side, to a stile at the end and then on alongside a tiny stream. Keep straight on at a small confluence in a corner, now following a lesser stream towards the edge of a wood. Before reaching it, a bridge crosses the stream to a stile behind. Entering a vast field, bear steadily left to meet the hedge, which conceals a green trackway. Pass a hollowed pool and keep on to a stile at the end, which admits to the old lane. Hereabouts it is somewhat overgrown, and the path merely crosses it.

Just down the other side a string of modern barns occupies the line of the path. Take the gate to the left of the first one, from where a broad track heads past the rest to emerge onto Church Lane in Great Mitton. Turn left, the road winding round to the junction at the centre of this tiny village.

Great Mitton offers refuge to all: along to the right is the Three Fishes *inn, while on the very corner is a tearoom. The church of All Hallows with its superb old*

tower dates from the 14th century. Inside is a splendid pre-Reformation screen which came from Sawley Abbey, while the Shireburn family chapel dates from 1594 and boasts an amazing assembly of recumbent effigies. A small grassy sward occupied by a seat tops it off, all in all making Great Mitton a place to break journey. Adjacent to the church is the rough-cast Old Hall with its mullioned windows. It too dates back in part to the 14th century, though is not best seen from this angle.

Great Mitton is truly a Yorkshire outpost: here the all-embracing West Riding - which extends remarkably to beyond Sheffield - burrows deep into the heart of Lancashire. Both Ribble and Hodder, which meet just downstream, form the true county boundary. **At the junction go left past the church and down the road to cross Mitton Bridge.** *Here the Ribble glides over low rocky shelves downstream, while upstream it leads the eye to Pendle Hill. Note also, while crossing, the fine setting of Great Mitton's old hall and church on their knoll - the mullioned and transomed east wall of the house is particularly well seen now.*

At the bridge end is the Aspinall Arms, its traditional inn sign, recalling a once important local family, echoed more individually on the front of the building itself. *Immediately past the pub is a stile, with Ribble Way signs pointing us upstream. The thin path follows the field edge to the far end, deflected by a wooded bank above the river. A further field-side leads on to a footbridge over a beck, then entering a large riverside pasture. Cross to the aqueduct bridge ahead. A track leads from a waterworks building for the latter stage to the bridge.* This shapely structure would look quite in keeping with its surrounds were it not for the material and colour!

Continue upstream on a broad track leading to Shuttleworth Farm. Passing left of the first building, their drive is followed out past several houses - the curiously named Fishes and Peggy Hill -and continues upstream beneath a well screened refuse site. The river here disappears in a great bow. Our road heads straight on, absorbing the 'tip' road. Just past the lone Mill House here, an unofficial but popular path slips into the trees on the left, following the beck upstream to escape the tip waggons in style. It rejoins the road at a stone arched bridge.

Just beyond, turn left along the drive towards Siddows Farm. At the early fork, go right a few yards then take a kissing-gate,

crossing a small field to one at the far corner. From here a path slants down to the river, which is followed upstream back to the start. On gaining the riverbank there is no suggestion of the proximity of civilisation, though soon people are likely to be encountered in great numbers. A well screened caravan site precedes the popular riverside picnic area, passing a miniature railway (Ribble Valley Live Steamers) en route. Toilets too, and a cafe. It's all here!

All Hallows,
Great Mitton:
Pendle Hill behind

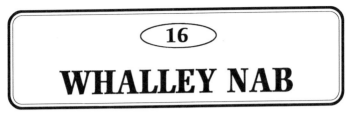

16

WHALLEY NAB

START Whalley   Grid ref. SD 732361

DISTANCE 5 miles

ORDNANCE SURVEY MAPS
1:50,000
Landranger 103 - Blackburn & Burnley
1:25,000
Pathfinder 680 - Longridge & Great Harwood

ACCESS Start from the town centre. There is a central car park. Whalley has a station on the Blackburn-Clitheroe line, and is also served by bus from various towns. An alternative start is the Spring Wood car park above the town, near the end of the walk (Grid ref. SD 740360).

Whalley is best known for its once influential abbey: the ruins are open to the public (entry fee). It was founded by Cistercian monks from Cheshire in 1296, though it took over a century to complete. Its last abbot, John Paslew, was hanged in 1536 for his involvement in the Pilgrimage of Grace. The massive building west of the ruins is the lay brothers' dormitory, which has seen various uses in the intervening years. More recent buildings are used as a diocesan conference centre, and in the grounds are a teashop, gift shop, visitor centre, toilets and a picnic area. The entrance is through the grand North-east Gatehouse, which dates from 1480.

Perhaps the finest feature at Whalley, however, is the magnificent early 14th century West Gatehouse which still hovers over the road: look up to savour the superb rib-vaulting. It is in the care of English Heritage. Next door to the abbey is the parish church of St. Mary & All Saints. Its proud features include a Norman south doorway, and early 15th century stalls that came from the abbey. In the churchyard are three 9th-11th century crosses. Within the old Square, opposite, are many old cottages, some Jacobean.

In more recent times a notable resident was the late Tom Stephenson, for 21 years secretary of the Ramblers' Association and a revered champion of walkers' rights: he was also the man behind Britain's first long-distance path, the Pennine Way.

☐ **From the mini-roundabout by the Dog Inn in the centre, turn down the road to cross the river by Whalley Bridge.** The river here is the Calder, not the Ribble. Downstream is a fine picture of the Whalley Viaduct. Known locally as 'Whalley Arches', this massive red brick viaduct dates from 1850 and comprises of around 50 arches. **Across the bridge, turn immediately up a steep lane through the trees. At the first opportunity, turn off to the left at a bend on a sunken bridleway. This soon reaches a viewpoint with a seat high above the winding river.**

The fork here is incidental, for footpath and bridleway run parallel through the wooded sliver to rejoin at the bottom of Nab Wood. Here turn right on a thin path along the wood bottom to reach a drive. This too is a fine viewpoint over the town, with Longridge Fell prominent, and a glimpse of the Bowland moors and part of Pendle. **Cross straight over to a stile and along the fence outside the trees. At the end turn up with it, quickly reaching a brow under the wooded Nab top.** Here views south and east open out, revealing the country to be traversed backed by the Burnley valley. Keep straight on towards the buildings that appear ahead. In the corner a stile admits to the corner of a garden. Keep straight on along the side to join the drive, which is followed out onto a narrow lane. Over to the east, Spence Moor is well seen.

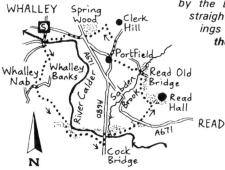

Turn left down the lane until just past another new house, then take a gate on the right to turn down the edge of the lawn. At the bottom a tiny footbridge leads into a plantation. The path runs through to emerge by a lonely oak into a newly planted section: here turn down to the left to join a cart track. Cross straight over and down to locate *a stile in the fence below. Life is simpler now as you head straight down the field to a barn below. A stile admits to an enclosed track. Cross straight over, past the barn and down to the bottom corner. Turn downstream with a tiny beck, and at the end we are ushered into crossing it. Continue down 50 yards, re-crossing on a slab bridge on a tiny confluence. A path of sorts now contours across the field.* The river Calder is looking good just below. *At the end of the field drop down above a forlorn ruin to approach a side-beck.*

A big slab bridge leads into the trees, and a path climbs the steep bank to run on above a superb bend of the river. At the end is a seat, and from the stile the way runs more freely along the top of the trees. Here one could be anywhere: wooded banks, swift flowing river, park-like surrounds... *At the end a path descends to the bank, crosses a side-stream and heads upstream. Beyond another side-stream the way is soon deflected up a part wooded bank, and then runs across the field to join the A680 Accrington road.* Just along to the right refreshment is available at the Gamecock inn.

The route turns left down the pavement to cross the river by Cock Bridge. Downstream is a splendid picture as the Calder leads the eye to Whalley Nab. *Across, turn right along the drive to a garden centre. At the end bear left on the cart track, rising pleasantly alongside Cock Wood.* Over to the right above the river is the defunct Martholme Viaduct on the former Blackburn-Padiham line. *Our track rises to join the A671. Cross straight over and up past the lodge on the drive to Read Hall.* Rising through attractive Read Park, only the merest glimpse of the hall itself is obtained through its surround of trees. Read Hall has strong links with the Pendle Witch stories: it was the home of Squire Roger Nowell, the local magistrate. The present hall was built in the 1820's.

On reaching the trees of Coppy Plantation, turn off the forking drive and take a stile on the left. A green track heads away outside the wood. Ahead again is Whalley Nab. *Remain on the track all the way, through several fields to descend towards Read Old Bridge. Join the road here and turn down over the bridge.* This was the scene of a Civil War skirmish between Royalists and local Roundheads in 1643. Upstream is the deep-cut dean of Sabden Brook.

Just up the other side turn along Easterly farm drive, but leave at the first chance by an early stile on the right. Ascend to the brow, then cross past a hollow to a stile ahead. The crest makes a splendid viewpoint, featuring Wiswell Moor, Spence Moor, Padiham

Heights, Longridge Fell and part of the Bowland moors. **Head straight across the next field, bound for the group of houses at Portfield.** Scanning the line of houses to the trees on the left, an obvious artificial bank identifies the outline of an Iron age hillfort. **Bear to the right in a smaller field then up another brow to reach a stile by the right-hand house, emerging onto a road junction.** Just along to the left is a barn conversion with a difference: it was originally a 14th century tithe barn of the monks of Whalley Abbey.

Turn right then left on the 'no through road'. Just past the golf club drive is a stile on the left. Slant up the field to a prominent skyline stile, then on past a massive hollow. Approaching a fence, turn down its near-side and descend to the bottom corner, with Spring Wood just to the right. A footbridge leads onto the edge of the golf course, going down outside the wood to join the main road. The car park is just to the right. An unofficial link path scurries across the beck just short of the bottom to lead directly to the picnic area.

Spring Wood car park has toilets, picnic site, and a labyrinth of paths winding through the trees. These are well worth a potter, especially at bluebell time. **To leave, cross the dual carriageway at the traffic lights and head straight down the side road to Whalley. At the 'Whalley' sign, take a path on the left that runs pleasantly down to the riverbank. This leads downstream, and at the weir - a nice spot - joins a rough lane to lead back out onto the street.**

North-east Gatehouse,
Whalley Abbey

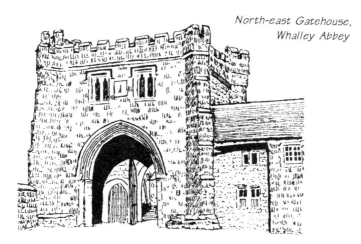

(17)

HODDER BRIDGES

START Higher Hodder Bridge   Grid ref. SD 697410

DISTANCE 4 miles

ORDNANCE SURVEY MAPS
1:50,000
Landranger 103 - Blackburn & Burnley
1:25,000
Pathfinder 669 - Clitheroe & Chipping
680 - Longridge & Great Harwood

ACCESS   Start from Higher Hodder Bridge: reasonable
parking at the Clitheroe end. Lower Hodder Bridge (mid-walk)
can be reached by Clitheroe-Longridge bus.

☐ *Head back up the road to the* **Hodder Bridge Hotel** *(closed at the time of publication) and turn right on a drive running along to several houses. Ahead is the Big End of Pendle, with Longridge Fell's eastern end behind, over your shoulder. Keep straight on to a gate at the end, and head off with an abandoned sunken way. At the bottom corner is a stile, just beneath which a stone footbridge crosses a tiny beck. Up the other side the old way, partly overgrown, curves away to the left, and part-way up a stile transfers us into the field alongside. Rising by the tree-lined stream, a stile at the top empties onto a road. In view back over to the left now are some of the Bowland moors, with Totridge prominent.*

With verges most of the way, turn right here to a T-junction. Go right 50 yards to the end of the trees, and take a stile into the field. Head diagonally away past a couple of oak trees to join the fence enclosing the wooded bank of the Hodder at the other side. There is a good full-length prospect of Pendle over to the left now. Go left with the fence to a corner stile, where a path runs through the belt of trees extending up from the bank. At the end resume as before, finally dropping to a stile onto the road at Lower Hodder Bridge. Turn right over the bridge. With one eye on traffic look downstream to the three arches of the remarkable Cromwell's Bridge, so named as the great historical figure passed this way prior to the Battle of Preston in 1648: it was built by one of the Shireburn family in the 16th century. Upstream is a lovely prospect of the Hodder.

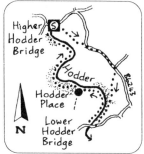

Across the bridge turn upstream, quickly leaving the drive to gain the riverbank. This is followed unerringly round a big sweep of the Hodder beneath the splendour of Hodder Place high above. A track forms to rise beneath a massive stone wall to approach the house. Formerly a junior school for Stoneyhurst which is located just along the lane (see WALK 18), Hodder Place has more recently been converted to flats. **When the track turns left for it, keep straight on a broad path descending into woodland. Immediately after a stream crossing is a divergance of paths. Our way tackles the great flight of wooden steps, climbing to a crossroads of paths. Though the way then embraces the next flight of steps, first go right for 50 yards to visit a stone cross, erected at a lovely spot high above another great sweep of the Hodder. Above the flight of steps, the path runs on the highest point of the bank, with the river far below.** These environs are as good a place as any to encounter deer.

At the wood corner a final flight takes us back down into the heart of the wood, meeting the abandoned original path midway. Turning left here, a grand walk ensues, quickly slanting down to approach the water's edge. Several well placed footbridges ease the way as the path emerges onto open grassy bank. Delightful walking leads round further bends to re-enter woodland. The last leg is a well constructed pathway through the trees, with the arches of Higher Hodder Bridge appearing ahead. The path passes to the right of a house before debouching by way of a footbridge and a well worn stone flight onto the road. Cross the bridge to finish.

Cromwell's Bridge

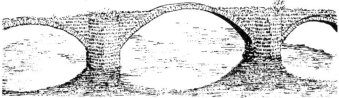

18

THREE RIVERS

START Hurst Green   Grid ref. SD 685379

DISTANCE 5 miles

ORDNANCE SURVEY MAPS
1:50,000
Landranger 103 - Blackburn & Burnley
1:25,000
Pathfinder 680 - Longridge & Great Harwood

ACCESS Start from the green in the village centre. Hurst Green is served by buses from Clitheroe, Chipping, Longridge and Preston.

Hurst Green is a pleasant village indelibly linked with nearby Stoneyhurst, of which more later in the walk. Near the wide junction in the village centre are the Post office/store, three pubs, and public toilets. The Eagle & Child *has 'Nuttalls' windows recalling a defunct Lancashire brewery, while the* Shireburn Arms *recalls the family that owned Stoneyhurst: morning coffee and afternoon tea are on offer, and a nice touch is a 'walkers welcome' sign. Indeed, Hurst Green is a popular venue for Lancashire ramblers. There is a war memorial on the green, while the cross over the road is a Boer War memorial. The modest little church of St John the Evangelist, further west along the road, dates from 1838.*

❏ *From the war memorial cross the main road and turn into the car park of the* Shireburn Arms. *Bearing down to the left, a short-lived green way leads to a wall-stile by a gate. Descend the field with the hedge, enjoying views over the valley, with Pendle to the left. When the fence turns off right, cross the fledgling stream and resume on a well defined tongue between miniature streams. From a stile at the bottom a path heads off through a band of trees, bearing left outside a wood to find a stile at the end. Here the path descends through woodland to a bridge over a side-stream. Beyond this the riverbank is gained, and the Ribble followed upstream. At once the graceful arches of an aqueduct are passed.* Ahead, the great bulk of Pendle Hill is dominant, and will remain in view for much of the walk.

The way is now foolproof for some time, as we trace the riverbank upstream. Just before joining a drive look back up to the left. The cross on the brow is a 19th century shaft in an older base. The drive leads to the farm at Jumbles. Without entering, turn right on the track to quickly regain the riverbank, and continue upstream. The modest scars that break the river's flow are known as Jumble Rocks. *A great loop of the river now ensues. A stile in a kink of the hedge gains the riverbank proper, with the splendid Hacking Hall directly ahead.* With its imposing five gables this hoary old place dates from 1607. Though not immediately apparent, it stands on the opposite bank.

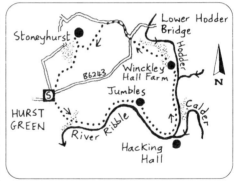

The old building we approach just ahead is the former boatman's house. This was in regular use when the Hacking Ferry plied the river. A small passenger boat operated well into the 1950's, and after a recent discovery in a barn, one of the old ferryboats was restored and is on display in the Castle Museum, Clitheroe. *Just beyond the old house make for the riverbank, where a seat bequeathed by the late Jessica Lofthouse awaits you and your sandwiches.*

Jessica Lofthouse was many people's favourite Lancashire author, having written countless topographical works on this and the surrounding counties. Her eye for history and detail, and her ability to put her story across in such a readable manner were unsurpassed. This idyllic spot is well favoured, being a perfect vantage point for the old hall, and also overlooking the confluence of the Calder with the Ribble. These are also favourite angling waters.

Resuming upstream, further riverside rambling leads to a track which comes in. *Over to the left are the cupolas of Stoneyhurst beneath Longridge Fell.* **The track takes us along to Winckley Hall Farm.** *Just prior to this is a vantage point where we part company with the Ribble, as it turns away with the Big End of Pendle directly behind. Approaching the farm, the realisation that we still have a river for company will catch out those not doing their homework, for the lovely Hodder now glides quietly alongside.*

Turn into the farmyard, past the big house. *Little remains of its Elizabethan origins, though some old windows hide round the back. The lovely L-shaped pond is the remains of a moat.* **Rise up the drive. Outside the grounds of Winckley Hall, take an iron kissing-gate on the right and cross straight over the field to another. Here a second field is crossed to the far-right corner: if the field is ploughed up the farmer's request is to tread the broad grassy verge of the headland round to the right.** *Part-way along, on the brow, the copper domed cupolas of Stoneyhurst return, rising across the fields.* **From the stile two short field-sides lead to a road junction.**

A longer alternative here turns down the road on a footway to Lower Hodder Bridge, then accompanies WALK 17 upstream to Hodder Place and thence to Stoneyhurst Post office.

From the bus shelter head straight up the the lane until just short of the Post office/store. Just to the left a broad driveway heads away to Hall Barn Farm. En route the college sports fields are passed. Don't enter the farmyard, but keep straight on a green way to a junction of ways. Here turn up the lane to the right to approach the college itself. Just before the wood on the left a gate is our route of departure, but first advance a little further along to savour the delights of the college. *First sighting is the chapel, with the South front just to the right. Ahead are the West front and the ponds.*

Stoneyhurst College is one of the country's leading Catholic boys' schools, with a long history in a beautiful setting. This impressive facade is, on closer inspection, a careful blend of old and not so old. The original Stoneyhurst of the Lords Shireburn began in the late 14th century. Their Elizabethan manor house was started by Sir Richard Shireburn, and the gatehouse dates from 1592. The family line was lost in 1717, and after neglect and change of ownership it was handed to the Society of Jesus in 1794. Coincidentially they had founded the 'English College' in northern France in 1593, and the invitation to take Stonyhurst came as they were experiencing difficulties under the French regime. The church of St Peter was built in 1832-35. In the mid-19th century much extension work took place, including the West front (1843-56) at the old gate-house, and the South block (1877-89). Cromwell is supposed to have stayed the night before the Battle of Preston in 1648.

Facing the West front are two serene ponds beloved of waterfowl, flanking the main drive which leads out along a broad avenue to a statue on the hill beyond: St Nicholas' Avenue was created between 1690 and 1717. The classic, main approach to the house, today it is a public road from just past the ponds, swinging round to the road we left at the other drive. The school is open to visitors (admission fee) on afternoons in the main Summer holidays, though the only Monday is at the bank holiday. In addition to the architectural features and all-round history, the house has count-less priceless treasures. The gardens are open at the same times, but start earlier in July. There is also a teashop and gift shop.

Back at the gate, head off along the long narrow field, transferring to the wooded side and then curving round past the end of the wood to an iron kissing-gate. Advance to the next such gate, then at the third, don't go through, but follow the hedge slanting away. At a wall (yes, a drystone wall) follow it round to the left to reach the head of a rough lane. Just beyond, it broadens to emerge back into the village centre.

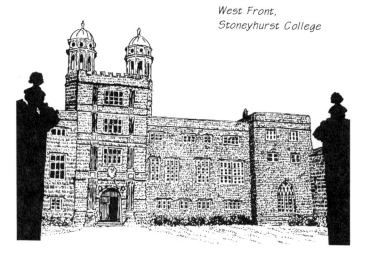

West Front,
Stoneyhurst College

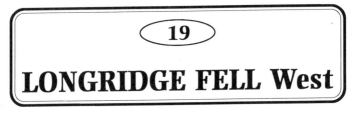

START   Loud Mytham   Grid ref. SD 648430

DISTANCE   6½ miles

ORDNANCE SURVEY MAPS
1:50,000
Landranger 103 - Blackburn & Burnley
1:25,000
Pathfinder 669 - Clitheroe & Chipping

ACCESS Start from Loud Mytham Bridge. There is room for several cars on the east side. One could also start from Doeford Bridge, just down the road. An alternative start is the mid-point of the walk, the Jeffrey Hill car park at Cardwell House on the upper slopes of Longridge Fell (GR 639401). The only snag is the walk's fine views are exposed before the first steps are even taken; and the first mile is steeply downhill!

Loud Mytham is a peaceful spot where the unassuming river Loud is absorbed by the Hodder: the main river is seen by a stroll down to Doeford Bridge. Loud Mytham Hall, by the bridge, is a most impressive 17th century house with mullioned windows.

☐ **Head up the Chipping road from the bridge, and within a few yards take a stile on the left. Climb the field-side above a pleasant wooded dell, and a farm track forms to lead up to a road by Wood Top Farm. Go left to the roadside farm at Cherry Tree House. Ignore the path opposite, and continue 100 yards to a gate on the right. Head up the field, veering right, through a line of old fenceposts to a stile in a kink at the top.** Longridge Fell looms above now, and the direct path slanting up it is unmistakable. **Resume up the field-side, bearing right to a hedge where a track forms. This doubles back left to Weedacre Farm, but pass through the gate and continue up to a couple of gates onto the road. Go left past the farm.**

The shorter route up the fell starts at a gate just yards past the house, reversing a section of WALK 20 as far as the summit wall near the OS column.

The main route goes past Weedacre Farm and another house before reaching the drive to Rakefoot. Follow this steeply up, and as it swings left towards the farm, take a bridle-gate on the right, and slant up the field to the prominent hollowed way above. This runs through the top corner of a field to a gate onto the foot of the fell proper. In deep sunken fashion it rises through newer plantings. *There are far more trees than the map shows, as will shortly be emphasised.*

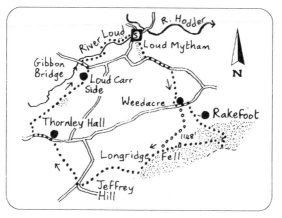

If not done so already, pause at an incoming path on a bend to survey the magnificent scene behind. The Bowland fells rise impressively across the Vale of Loud, with Chipping boasting an idyllic setting beneath the steep moorland slopes. Over to the left is the island-like Beacon Fell, while Parlick blends in with the main body of Bowland fells. Around to the right, the more distant peaks of Ingleborough and Penyghent in the Yorkshire Dales make their entrance. The Big End of Pendle makes a brief appearance before trees impinge. **The way is infallible as it breasts the slopes, eventually curving round to run on to a level fork.**

Bear right, soon running on between the trees to reach a broad forest road. Without actually joining it, turn immediately right on the more inviting, right-hand concessionary path that heads back through the trees. This quickly runs along to approach the end of

the old wall that runs the length of the felltop. Pass through a gap and head away to the left, many of the wall's old stones having been requisitioned to strengthen the path. The way runs clearly on, through trees that further impede the view north with each passing year, to reach a stile at a staggered wall junction. With open moor on the right now, a broad track runs on towards the Ordnance column that has appeared ahead. A path also runs on the right side of the wall, through a gap.

For more on Longridge Fell, please refer to WALK 20. **Leaving, remain with the wall to reach a path junction at a stile where the direct path gains the felltop. Resume with the wall again, on to a stile in a fence and then on a direct march along the fell.** Our way runs by sweeping heather with distant views out over the Longridge reservoirs to Preston and the coast. **When the plantation on the left ends, there is a choice of ways. The current path remains with the wall all the way to emerge onto a road, which followed right leads to the Jeffrey Hill car park at Cardwell House. The main route leaves the clear path here, and crosses to the minor depression on the right, between a reedy area and a row of shooting hides. Waymarking sees us across the outflowing stream and along a clearer path to the left.** This is a concessionary path made available by agreement with the landowner.

The path contours above the steeper northern scarp, fading as heather gives way to short-cropped turf. Bear left here, one or two stone marker posts confirming the route. A tractor track forms to curve around and show the way to a kissing-gate off the moor to the car park. If you started here, then that's it! Those starting here will be stunned by the views before even pulling their boots on. Whilst the undoubted highlight is the mass of Bowland fells across Chipping's fertile vale, the Dales mountains beyond feature a fine array from Ingleborough to Great Whernside.

Approaching the car park drop down to the road junction beneath the sharp bend. Go right a few yards and take a stile on the left. Descend the field. Almost at once we cross the line of the Roman road from Ribchester to Over Burrow in the Lune Valley. **Bear left to the bottom of a row of trees enshrouding a tiny stream on the left. Skirt round the fence corner below (not as per map) and descend between stream and fence to join the road opposite Thornley Hall. Go left past the farm, five minutes down the road to the first drive on the right. Turn down this to a small cluster of dwellings.**

Immediately before the large house on the right take an easily missed stile and head along the bottom of the field, past the house and on to a rickety stile. *Longridge Fell itself has now become part of the view, the broad ridge running along to our right.* **Continuing, cross to a sturdy stile in a section of wall, and straight on to the edge of the plantation of Park Wood. Bear left outside it, along two field-sides to a tiny footbridge. Bear left towards the house - Loud Carr Side - behind, entering and leaving its paddock by step-stiles. At the barn, go left through the gate and follow the drive out onto the road. Go left a short way to reach Gibbon Bridge.** *Just across is the* Gibbon Bridge *hotel, where in addition to refreshments you can take advantage of a beauty salon.*

Don't cross the bridge - unless feeling ugly - but take a stile to follow the river Loud downstream. *This is a lovely section, the Loud being the most unassuming of burbling streams.* **At the end of the second field is a footbridge over a side-stream, and a ruin and an anglers' hut behind. Here at Bailey Hippings we hope to cross the river.** *Hippings are stepping stones, and in times of spate this is unlikely to be a successful venture, though normally the ten or so massive stones are steady enough.* **Assuming a safe crossing, turn downstream, and the way resumes very pleasantly through several rickety stiles down to Loud Mytham Bridge, finishing at a stile by a gate just up from the bridge.**

Meanwhile, back at the stones: unfortunately, there is no right of way any further down the east bank, the clear and obvious way being only an anglers' path. If baulked, re-cross the footbridge and turn upstream to join the road by a junction. Turn left, and at another junction left again to drop down to Loud Mytham.

Ordnance Survey column, Longridge Fell, looking to Ingleborough and Penyghent

LONGRIDGE FELL East

START Hurst Green   Grid ref. SD 685379

DISTANCE 8½ miles

ORDNANCE SURVEY MAPS
1:50,000
Landranger 103 - Blackburn & Burnley
1:25,000
Pathfinder 669 - Clitheroe & Chipping
               680 - Longridge & Great Harwood

ACCESS Start from the green in the village centre. Hurst Green is served by Clitheroe-Longridge buses.

This superb walk has little in the way of less inspiring sections: the approach to Longridge Fell is outstanding, and the rewards commensurate. The return skirts round the fell, rather than re-ascending. For a note on Hurst Green, please refer to page 74.

☐ **Leave the village on Avenue Road, from the war memorial opposite the** Shireburn Arms. **On reaching the** Bayley Arms, **consider a small detour.** *Just past the pub and village hall is the Shireburn Almshouse, an impressive building with various inscriptions and arms, and splendid semi-circular steps. Built in 1706, it was transferred here from Kemple End after World War Two.* **From the pub, meanwhile, a footpath sign opposite points down a drive on the left. Pass right of the garages at the bottom, and a woodland path runs on to meet another drive: the same applies, running on to re-enter woodland.**

With Dean Brook for company, the path quickly joins a broader pathway at some waterfalls, and the ensuing stage is a wonderful walk with the finest combination of woodland and water scenery. Stone arched Sandy Bridge takes us over the beck. *Be sure to view the waterslides and falls just upstream.* **The way then rises left, out along the top of the trees and into open surroundings.** *Ahead is the long line of Longridge Fell plastered in conifers: it has its better side!*

This smashing green way runs on, rising and receiving a more durable surface before joining a broad driveway. This rises to **Greengore, the farm just ahead.** *Its intriguing architecture includes novel buttresses: it dates back several centuries and was at one time a hunting lodge.* **Keep straight on up, right of the buildings, and a track continues with lovely woodland to the right. The track soon turns into the trees, but remain outside the wall on a super path.**

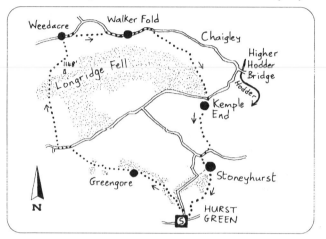

The path runs on beyond the wood, soon reaching a deer fence at a new plantation on the left. **From the gate at the end, forsake the track, and bear left up the field. Aim between the plantation on the right and the natural wood to its left, to find a ladder-stile in between.** *Look back over the cupolas of Stonyhurst and beyond the Ribble to a skyline of the West Pennine moors and Pendle Hill.* **Slant up again to the brow.** *This grand moment reveals the western half of Longridge Fell now living up to its name. Here also is a recumbent boundary stone inscribed 'B'.*

Slant down to the far corner, and from the stile slant up the field to a stile onto a road. Go left a short way to an inviting drive. *A highly individual sign confirms that while this area might be overlooking the Ribble, it is in truth Bowland in nature.* **Turn up the drive, rising past all the names on the board and with improving views over the fell to the left. At the top the drive finally turns for the last house, Moor Game Hall: keep straight on up a short-lived grassy way onto a corner of the moor. A modest but grand path continues the climb, through increasing heather to a wall junction**

at the top. It then slants to the right, in deeper heather to reach a forest track. Crossing straight over, the path runs on through younger plantings to gain the wall running along the crest of the fell.

From the ladder-stile the path goes forward again. *First, however, one will be stopped in one's tracks by the prospect ahead: the Bowland moors are arrayed in total splendour, a prospect worth every step of this walk. From Beacon Fell round to Waddington Fell, the wonderful heights of Parlick, Fair Snape and Totridge front this upland dome. Its foreground complements it, with the wooded meanderings of the Hodder traced through green fields liberally scattered with farms. The village of Chipping is evident towards the foot of Parlick.* ***Though not essential to the view, normal practice is to detour to the Ordnance column on the right, on Spire Hill.***

At 1148ft this marks the summit of the most southerly named fell in the country, and is clearly a place of pilgrimage for West Lancashire walkers. The column (S4561) sits atop a concrete plinth, and brings in a few other features to east and south - until the trees reach full height, at least. For such a modest height, Longridge offers a remarkable panororama. Its detachment from other high ground is the key, allied to the fact that the Bowland massif is so near: this is surely the finest vantage point for Bowland. All this, by the way, makes its own advertisement for the sister guidebook to BOWLAND!

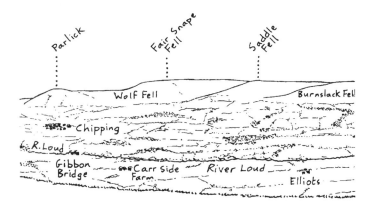

A sight for sore eyes: the Bowland moors from Longridge.

Returning to the path at the stile, advance over the edge to quickly gain an appreciation of the northern scarp of the fell. The path evades an ungainly plunge by swinging right to enjoy a civilised slant down the face. For the most part our path traces an old sunken way, to within yards of the wall at the bottom. In fact it points directly to a ladder-stile off the fell. Head down the field-side, meeting a marshy corner before a stile admits to a broad, enclosed way. This leads down to a gate onto a road at Weedacre Farm. Turn right for a few minutes, being aware that this country road sees its fair share of traffic.

Just past a bridleway leading up the drive to Rakefoot, take a stile on the right opposite a house. Climb the field-side to a stile onto a green way encased in foliage. Go left along this, initially less appealing though there is chance to escape into the field top alongside. The way soon improves, though one or two nettle-filled sections again call for escape. Beyond a tiny stream the hollowed way ends abruptly, and a stile ahead sees us resume along the field-tops. With the Craven Heifer *inn in view ahead, cross the last field directly to it, turning left in its garden to emerge back onto the road.*

After possible refreshment resume along the road to the tiny hamlet of Walker Fold. On the right a tiny plaque informs about the old Walker Fold school and chapel. A Victorian postbox, a seat and a phone box are also passed. *Remain on the road a short while longer, and just past a couple of cottages, take a gate at a footpath*

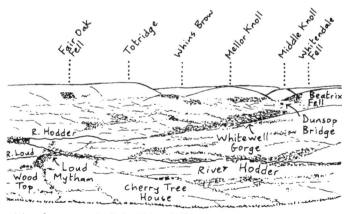

with a foreground of the Vale of Chipping and Little Bowland

sign on the right. *Slant across this domed field to the tree-lined stream opposite, and just short of the top corner, cross it to a faint grassy trackway alongside. Pass through a gateway and head away above a fence. There is a dark wall of conifers up to the right now. The next but one stile is found not in the corner, but a little to the right: from it take up with a fence on the right to head towards farm buildings visible ahead.*

Just before a stream in the corner, take a stile on the right and resume above the marshiness near the fence. Aim to the right of the barn and ruin of Chaigley Hall, and head away with a fence slanting up to the foot of the plantation. Without entering, the path now runs along the base of the woods, encountering stiles in various states. A memorial seat to a Liverpool rambler is passed in this discerning location. *Continuing, a broad track is soon joined above a barn at Turner Fold, and an attractive section leads along the foot of the wood and out onto the steeply climbing road at Kemple End.* This is a colourful corner, with open country and old quarries draped in heather, bilberry and bracken.

Cross over and along a drive, which swings round to approach a private looking drive. Keep straight on past the house to discover several more enviable dwellings scattered about. Keep on towards the end, then turn left on the track as it swings round to some farm buildings. At the last barn a short-lived farm lane leads out into a field: a stile on the left by the last barn offers the chance to avoid any muddiness. If using it, keep to the field top and down the far side a little to another stile: full marks to someone for this. *Emerging into the field, cross to the fence on the left and head away, passing a minor indentation to reach a stile at the end, under hawthorns. From it head down the field-side, keeping an eye out for a stile part-way down. From this descend another field-side towards the house at Throstle Nest below. A stile admits to its drive, which is followed out through the fields onto a road. Go right a short way, then turn down the drive to Stoneyhurst College. This leads down through the trees to the front of the college - a splendid moment.* For information on Stoneyhurst, please refer to page 76.

Continue past the chapel, and as the trees on the right end, head off from a gate on the right along the long, narrow field, moving to the wooded side and curving round past the end of the wood to an iron kissing-gate. Advance to the next such gate, then at the third don't go through, but follow a hedge slanting away. At a wall (yes, a drystone wall) follow it round to the left to reach the head of a rough lane. Just beyond, it broadens to emerge back in the village.

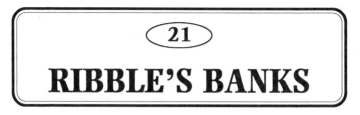

RIBBLE'S BANKS

START Marles Wood   Grid ref. SD 675356

DISTANCE 4¾ miles

ORDNANCE SURVEY MAPS
1:50,000
Landranger 103 - Blackburn & Burnley
1:25,000
Pathfinder 680 - Longridge & Great Harwood

ACCESS Start from Marles Wood car park near Salesbury Hall, on the Ribchester Bridge-Old Langho road. If using public transport, start from Ribchester Bridge, mid-route, which is crossed by Blackburn-Ribchester-Longridge buses.

An easy ramble through outstanding Ribble-side scenery.

☐ *At the car park entrance a notice informs that the Roman road from Ribchester to York (AD70) was exposed during construction work in 1992.* **A little path from the car park short-cuts the drive to join the road. Descend for 100 yards as far as a stile on the left, then head up the field outside Rhododendron Plantation. When the wood bends away at the top, bear right to locate a stile in the fence ahead. Continue slanting right to the top of the next field, arriving at a circular pond at the top.** *A glance at the Pathfinder map reveals a necklace of such pools scattered about the district. These are man-made to providing drinking water for the grazing beasts. They are now home to many species of damsel- and dragon-flies.*

Turn right at the pond to find a clear track running along the field-side, quickly passing a second pond - this fringed with irises - to arrive at the head of a lane just before the corner. Instead of turning down this green lane, turn right and head directly away from it, over the field to locate a stile at the other side. Then descend outside Park Wood, gently left on a broad tongue of land. *Ahead now is a* *fine prospect of the Ribchester district, with the Ribble Valley backed by the great whaleback of Longridge Fell. Directly below, the arches of Ribchester Bridge are in view.*

At the bottom bear left a little to find a footbridge, beyond which make a bee-line for the waiting hotel at Ribchester Bridge. Several fences are crossed by means of step-stiles before emerging into the car park. *The* De Tabley *inn currently includes a nightclub, so bring your disco gear for a swift change of scene on a summer evening ramble. Its name recalls an important landowning family. Two minutes along the road to the left is New Hall, a fine 17th century house with mullioned windows and a carving above the doorway.*

Ribchester Bridge, with its three graceful arches, dates from 1774. **Cross the bridge with care and turn along a farm drive upstream. This leaves the river part-way along to reach Dewhurst House. Entering the yard, turn down to the right to find a short-lived pathway that emerges onto the riverbank in a lovely setting. Turn**
upstream, remain-
ing on a sketchy
path generally close
to the river. Now
passing beneath
Stewart's Wood it
runs on to enter
Haugh Wood by
step-stile and foot-
bridge. *A glorious*
woodland section
ensues on the
bank, which here
undergoes a great
wide sweep.

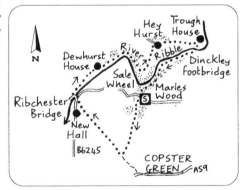

Just before the end the path swings up to the left to a stile out of the trees, and climbs the small bank into a field. Cross over the brow. *Here we are greeted by a superb panorama, with another fine sweep of the river leading the eye to the mass of Pendle Hill.* **Over to the left is Hey Hurst, for which we are bound, and a stile just down to the left is the key. From it a track of sorts slants up a sheep pasture, rising above the house to find a stile at the far corner. Cross a small enclosure to a stile onto the drive just above the house.**

Almost opposite, a stile sends us off again along the hedge-side, meeting a wood at the far end of the field and descending to a tiny footbridge at the bottom. From it follow the hedge directly away, along the bottom of several fields until a fence parts company. Here keep straight on a track to become enclosed, with the bold supports of Dinckley footbridge prominent just to the right. Approaching Trough House Farm, leave the track on a short and narrow pathway doubling back to the bridge.

Cross in style on this high suspension bridge, enjoying lovely views both up and down river. The far bank is the place for a repose, to partake of refreshment and take in the verdant loveliness. The bridge was erected in 1951, replacing the Dinckley Ferry which had previously operated. Just beneath the bridge a series of scars interrupt the water's flow, while herons are regularly sighted.

Turn downstream to enjoy the loveliest riverside section of this walk. Over to the left, in season, are great swaths of irises, with fine woodland increasingly encroaching. *An intervening field is crossed with the river obscured by trees, but at the other end a smashing prospect is revealed as the Ribble glides between richly wooded banks. Just downstream a stile admits to Marles Wood, and a gem of a path heads away. At the far end the rocks of Coppy Scar call for a further halt.* This aggressively attractive section of river features the whirlpool of Sale Wheel, before it turns away for some contrastingly lazy sweeps. *Our path bears left to remain in the trees, and an early branch left is a concessionary path climbing directly to the car park. Alternatively, remain on the right of way which, beyond a footbridge, itself quickly climbs away to emerge onto the road 130 yards below the car park.*

Ribchester Bridge

RIBCHESTER

START Ribchester   Grid ref. SD 650350

DISTANCE 6 miles

ORDNANCE SURVEY MAPS
1:50,000
Landranger 102 - Preston & Blackpool *or*
                103 - Blackburn & Burnley
1:25,000
Pathfinder 680 - Longridge & Great Harwood

ACCESS Start from the village centre, outside the *White Bull*. There is a large car park nearby. Ribchester is served by Blackburn-Longridge buses, and also from Preston.

Even without its Roman connections Ribchester is an interesting village. The Roman fort of BREMETENNACUM originated in AD 79 to guard an important river crossing on their road north from Manchester. The Roman Museum contains many relics, including a copy of a magnificent helmet found by the river 200 years ago: it is open throughout the year. Alongside is St. Wilfrid's church with its early 14th century tower: inside are a Jacobean pulpit and box pews dating from 1735.

The village contains 18th and 19th century cottages once busy with handloom weaving, and other attractive houses from various periods. One of several pubs is the White Bull, *dated 1707: its front columns have been claimed as Roman, though this is unlikely. A local speciality at the butchers is Ribchester sausage. Another award winner is the Museum of Childhood, open daily except Mondays: it also features a toyshop and refreshments.*

☐ *From the end of the main street above the riverbank, turn left on the footpath past the school. There is an immediate gorgeous prospect of the wide flowing Ribble. The path leads to the Roman bath house. The site is normally open to view. The path continues on, over a bridge and out onto a back road, Greenside. Turn right* to the junction opposite the **Ribchester Arms.** *Note the old 'Ribchester New Hotel' sign on the wall opposite.* **Turn right past the hotel, then sharply left up Stydd Lane.** *Up ahead is Longridge Fell.* **The drive runs up past a school to a fascinating corner.**

Here is St. Peter and St. Paul's Roman Catholic barn church dating from 1789. By the roadside are the delightful Stydd Almshouses. Built in 1728 by the Shireburn family of Stoneyhurst, the building still serves its original function. An open, curved staircase and pillared balcony are features of this recently modernised gem. **Continue up the now rough drive to the old church of St. Saviours.** *This old chapel dates from the 12th century, and belonged to a Preceptory of the Knights Hospitallers. It has two Norman windows and a doorway. An ancient cross base sits in the grass out front.*

The drive ends at the farm at Stydd Manor. *Above the doorway is*

a 1698 datestone. **Head straight up the yard, emerging via a couple of gates into the field behind. A rough track rises away with the hedge on the right. At a corner stile the track fades.** *Note a hollowed pool on the right. This is a dewpond created by farmers to quench their cattle's thirst. It is only the first of many passed in the next couple of miles: the Pathfinder map reveals the Ribchester area to be awash with them.*

Resume with a hedge on the left, to leave by a footbridge at the top corner. Up through a further stile, now slant over to a makeshift stile by a gate at the top corner. Up to the left is a communications mast. Above, the climb is completed by way of a pronounced sunken grassy way on the brow. *This highest point of the walk is favoured with extensive views, finest features being Longridge Fell directly ahead, and the whaleback of Pendle Hill to the right. Behind is a great sweep of the Ribble Valley backed by the West Pennine moors above Blackburn, and the South Pennines beyond Burnley.*

The part-sunken way runs on to a farmhouse at Duddel Hill. Pass to its left to follow the drive out onto the road. Without actually crossing the cattle-grid, however, turn sharp left across the field to a stile opposite. Continue to another then pass through a line of old hawthorns. As the field drops away at the end, aim for white-walled houses ahead and bear down to the right to find a footbridge over tree-lined Stydd Brook. Over the field behind, cross a tiny side-stream and rise to a gate to the left of the house at Cox Farm.

Go right a handful of yards along the road and take a stile on the left twixt holly hedges. Cross to another, on through a gateway in a hedge, then bear right to a corner stile. Head away with a hedge on the left to another corner stile, then bear across to the next field to the end of the row of trees on the right. A track forms to join a solid drive with Kellets Farm on the right. Go right only 20 or so yards, however, and take a stile on the left. Cross to the far corner of the field, between the two houses opposite. A stile admits to the corner of a garden at Scott House to join the back road.

Go left only another 30 or so yards and take a stile on the right. Descend by a winding hedge to a footbridge, then cross to a stile at the far side of the field. Though a tempting green pathway contours away, our way descends towards the brook. Just upstream is a stile admitting to the corner of another garden (extended from that on the map). Cross towards the house, bearing round to the left corner where a short enclosed path leads out, over a bridge alongside a ford. Go left along the lane to rise to a junction. Turn left here to a junction with the Ribchester-Longridge road at the Cross Keys inn at Ward Green Cross.

Turn right here, being spoiled for choice with footways on both sides. Cross with care, and leave by a part-hidden stile opposite a couple of bungalows and an agricultural garage. Follow a hedge away to the corner, and from the stile advance a few more yards to a stile on the right. Head away to the right with a fence now, and at the corner gate transfer to the other side to head along to Lord's Farm, just ahead. A short enclosed way passes the right side of the yard to follow the drive out onto a lane.

Go left down the lane, past Falicon Farm to a demise at Eatoughs Farm. Remain on the now grassy drive as it turns left, soon ending in a field. Maintain the direction, straight across the field to locate a stile at the far end, a little above the bottom corner. Through it, descend 100 yards right to a prominent hand-gate on a bridleway, and follow the left side of the field a short way round to a stile by a gateway. Go left along the field-side above the deep wooded confines of the beck. From a stile at the end, the beck parts company as we remain on the pronounced bank, passing a tall pylon to approach the clump of trees ahead. Just before then a curious drive, flanked by stone posts, is crossed.

The trees sit atop a steep bank, with the Ribble now revealed in its glory below: Pendle rises over to the left. *Our way goes left with the undiscernible Ribble Way, but first it is worth going right a few yards to the top of the bank to halt and savour the classic view, with the river winding lazily away beyond Hothersall Hall.*

Resuming, head down the left side of the wooded bank to a corner gate and follow the river upstream. From the next gate a fence ushers us away from the river. A track forms, becoming enclosed to run along to Boat House. This once served the ferry to Osbaldeston Hall. *The broad drive leads all the way back to the village.* In the early stages Osbaldeston Hall on the opposite bank is well seen. *Ribchester's church tower appears ahead, and the drive runs through the yard of Lower Alston Farm before emerging back on the riverbank at the end of the street where we began.*

Stydd Almshouses

SOME USEFUL ADDRESSES

Ramblers' Association 1/5 Wandsworth Road
London SW8 2XX   Tel. 0171-582 6878

Lancashire Countryside Service (Bowland AONB)
PO Box 160, East Cliff County Offices, Preston PR1 3EX
Tel. 01772-264709

North West Water (Recreation & Conservation Officer)
Pennine House, Stanley Street, Preston PR1 4EA
Tel. 01772-822200

Tourist Information

12-14 Market Place, **Clitheroe** BB7 2DA
Tel. 01200-25566

The Old Library, Fernlea Avenue, **Barnoldswick** Colne BB8 5DW
Tel. 01282-817046

Town Hall, Market Street, **Nelson** BB9 7LG
Tel 01282-692890

King George's Hall, Northgate, **Blackburn** BB2 1AA
Tel. 01254-53277

The Guildhall, Lancaster Road, **Preston** PR1 1HT
Tel. 01772-53731

Barley Information Centre Tel. 01282-601893

Bowland Camping Barns
YHA, 16 Shawbridge Street, Clitheroe, BB7 1LY
Tel. 01200-28366

Lancashire County Transport Information
County Surveyors Dept, Winckley House, PO Box 9, Cross
Street, Preston PR1 8RD   Tel. 01772-254868

British Rail, Blackburn-Clitheroe line Tel. 01200-443800

LOG OF THE WALKS

WALK	DATE	NOTES
1		
2		
3		
4		
5		
6		
7		
8		
9		
10		
11		
12		
13		
14		
15		
16		
17		
18		
19		
20		
21		
22		

INDEX

Principal features: walk number refers